For exams from September 2025 to December 2026

ICAEW
Business Insight and Performance

First edition 2025

ISBN 9781 0355 3082 3
eISBN 9781 0355 2954 4

British Library Cataloguing-in-Publication Data
A catalogue record for this book is available from the
British Library

Published by

BPP Learning Media Ltd,
BPP House, Aldine Place,
142–144 Uxbridge Road,
London W12 8AA

learningmedia.bpp.com

Printed in the United Kingdom

Your learning materials, published by BPP Learning
Media Ltd, are printed on paper obtained from traceable,
sustainable sources.

All rights reserved. No part of this publication may be
reproduced, stored in a retrieval system or transmitted, in any
form or by any means, electronic, mechanical, photocopying,
recording or otherwise, without the prior written permission of
BPP Learning Media.

NO AI TRAINING. Unless otherwise agreed in writing, the use of
BPP material for the purpose of AI training is not permitted. Any
use of this material to "train" generative artificial intelligence (AI)
technologies is prohibited, as is providing archived or cached
data sets containing such material to another person or entity.

The content of this publication is intended to prepare students for
the ICAEW examinations, and should not be used as professional
advice. Although every effort has been made to ensure that the
contents of this book are correct at the time of going to press, BPP
Learning Media makes no warranty that the information in this
book is accurate or complete and accepts no liability for any loss
or damage suffered by any person acting or refraining from acting
as a result of the material in this book.

ICAEW takes no responsibility for the content of any supplemental
training materials supplied by the Partner in Learning.

The ICAEW Partner in Learning logo, ACA and ICAEW CFAB are
all registered trademarks of ICAEW and are used under licence by
BPP Learning Media Ltd.

©
BPP Learning Media Ltd

Welcome to BPP Learning Media's **Passcards** for ICAEW **Business Insight and Performance**.

- They **save you time**. Important topics are summarised for you.
- They incorporate **diagrams** to kick start your memory.
- They follow the overall **structure** of the ICAEW Workbook, but BPP Learning Media's ICAEW **Passcards** are not just a condensed book. Each card has been separately designed for clear presentation. Topics are self-contained and can be grasped visually.
- ICAEW **Passcards** are **just the right size** for pockets, briefcases and bags.
- ICAEW **Passcards focus on the exams** you will be facing.

Run through the **Passcards** as often as you can during your final revision period. The day before the exam, try to go through the **Passcards** again! You will then be well on your way to passing your exams.

Good luck!

Preface | Contents

		Page			Page
1	Data analysis tools	1	8	Budgeting	83
2	Technology, ethics and sustainability	23	9	Working capital	97
3	The fundamentals of costing	39	10	Standard costing and variance analysis	113
4	Calculating unit costs (Part 1)	47	11	Breakeven analysis and limiting factor analysis	127
5	Calculating unit costs (Part 2)	55	12	Investment appraisal techniques	135
6	Marginal costing and absorption costing	63	13	The external environment of business	149
7	Pricing calculations	67			

1: Data analysis tools

Topic List

- Data and information
- Data analysis considerations
- Spreadsheets
- Charts
- Big data and data analytics
- Protection of commercially sensitive information

In this chapter, we look at how information is used in business, including qualities of information, types of data analysis and potential problems with data.

| Data and information | Data analysis considerations | Spreadsheets | Charts | Big data and data analytics | Protection of commercially sensitive information |

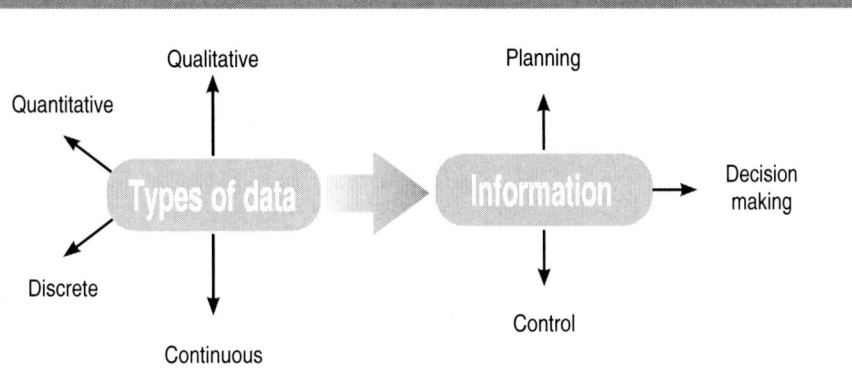

Internal data sources – eg, accounting records

External data sources – eg, government

Internet of things – devices that connect over the internet or a network to perform a range of tasks

Qualities of good information: ACCURATE

Accurate: Adding-up, rounding, error-free, properly categorised, state assumptions, identify uncertainty

Complete: Include everything needed, such as external data, comparatives

Cost-beneficial: Benefits of having information > costs of obtaining it; efficient collection and analysis

User-targeted: Needs of user should be met eg, detailed or summarised?

Relevant: Unnecessary information should be omitted

Authoritative: Reliable sources

Timely: Should be available when it is needed

Easy to use: Clear presentation; no longer than necessary; sent in appropriate form, medium and channel

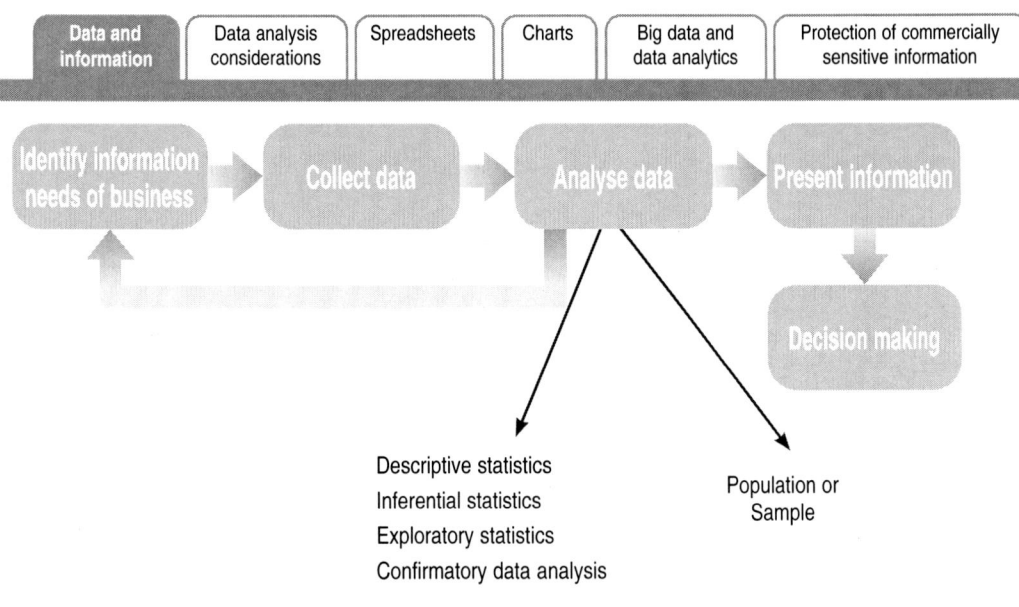

Representative samples

Reflect the characteristics of the population

Factors:

- Method of sample selection
- Sample size

Methods of sampling

- Simple random sampling
- Systematic sampling
- Stratified sampling

| Data and information | Data analysis considerations | Spreadsheets | Charts | Big data and data analytics | Protection of commercially sensitive information |

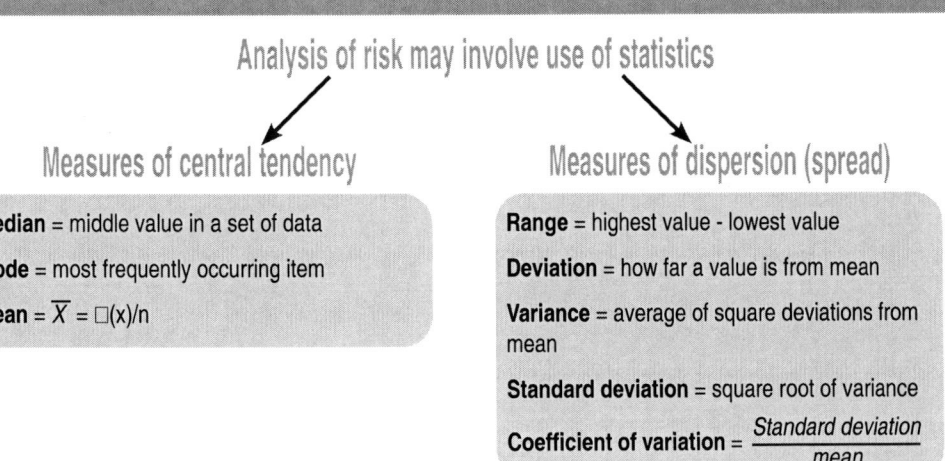

Analysis of risk may involve use of statistics

Measures of central tendency

Median = middle value in a set of data

Mode = most frequently occurring item

Mean = $\overline{X}$ = $\square(x)/n$

Measures of dispersion (spread)

Range = highest value - lowest value

Deviation = how far a value is from mean

Variance = average of square deviations from mean

Standard deviation = square root of variance

Coefficient of variation = $\dfrac{Standard\ deviation}{mean}$

Evaluation of measures

	Mean	**Median**	**Mode**
Advantages	<ul><li>Widely understood (average)</li><li>Representative of all values in data</li><li>Can be used in further statistical analysis</li></ul>	<ul><li>Easy to understand</li><li>Not distorted by outliers</li></ul>	<ul><li>Easy to find and understand</li><li>Will always take a value equal to an actual value in the data</li><li>Can be used for qualitative data</li><li>Not distorted by outliers</li></ul>
Disadvantages	<ul><li>Value may not be the same as any actual values in the data</li><li>May return same value for very different sets of data</li><li>May be distorted by outliers</li></ul>	<ul><li>Value may not be the same as any actual values in the data</li><li>Calculation of it does not use all data in data set therefore not representative</li><li>Difficult to identify in large data sets</li><li>Not suited to further statistical analysis</li></ul>	<ul><li>Calculation of it does not use all data in data set therefore not representative</li><li>Not suited to further statistical analysis</li></ul>

| Data and information | Data analysis considerations | Spreadsheets | Charts | Big data and data analytics | Protection of commercially sensitive information |

Normal distribution

Many large data sets approximate a normal distribution:

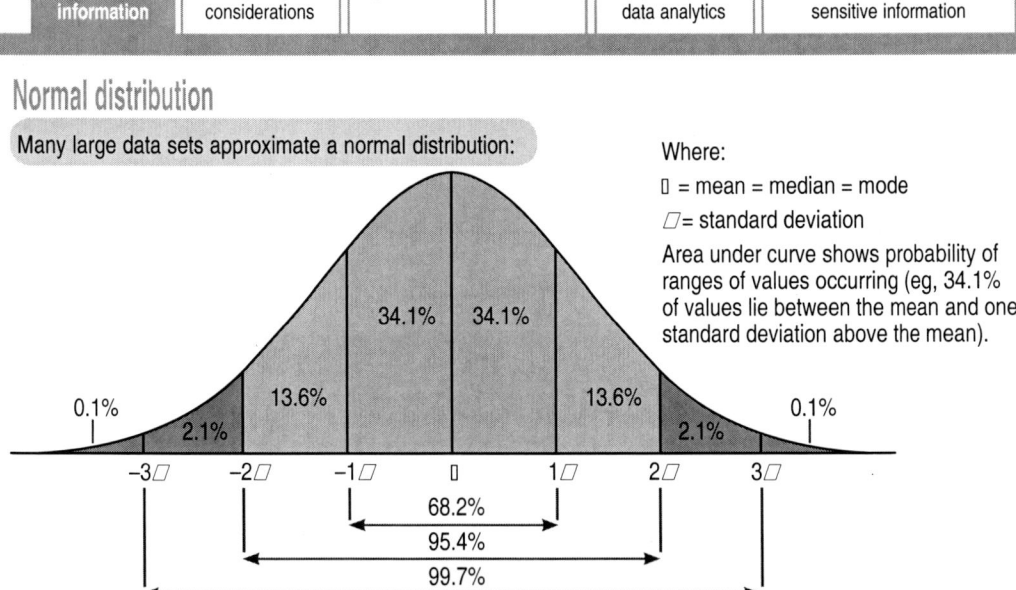

Where:

μ = mean = median = mode

σ = standard deviation

Area under curve shows probability of ranges of values occurring (eg, 34.1% of values lie between the mean and one standard deviation above the mean).

| Data and information | **Data analysis considerations** | Spreadsheets | Charts | Big data and data analytics | Protection of commercially sensitive information |

Professional scepticism: assessing information, estimates and explanations **critically** with a **questioning mind**, and **being alert to possible misstatements** due to error and fraud

Comparability: data not distorted by use of different definitions or measuring methods

Type I error – a **hypothesis is true** but is **rejected** because the sample result differs significantly from hypothesis

Type II error – a **hypothesis is false** but is **accepted** because the sample result is not significantly different from hypothesis

| Data and information | **Data analysis considerations** | Spreadsheets | Charts | Big data and data analytics | Protection of commercially sensitive information |

Linear regression analysis

is a statistical technique for establishing a straight line equation to represent a set of data.

Correlation

is the extent to which the value of a dependent variable is related to the value of the independent variable.

Perfect positive correlation

Partial correlation

Degrees of correlation

- Perfectly correlated
- Partly correlated
- Uncorrelated
- Non-linear or curvilinear correlation

Values of r

- $r = +1$ = perfect positive
- $r = -1$ = perfect negative
- $r = 0$ = uncorrelated

No correlation

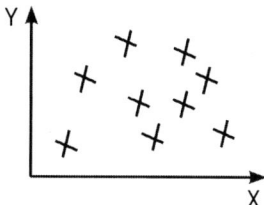

Non-linear or curvilinear correlation

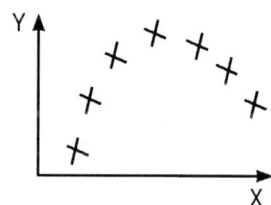

| Data and information | Data analysis considerations | Spreadsheets | Charts | Big data and data analytics | Protection of commercially sensitive information |

Coefficient of determination, r^2

r^2 measures the proportion of the total variation in the value of one variable that can be explained by variations in the value of the other variable.

If $r = 0.9$, $r^2 = 0.81$

If the correlation coefficient of two variables = 0.9, we know the variables are **positively correlated**. The coefficient of determination, $r^2 = 0.81$ and this gives a more meaningful analysis. We know that 81% of the variations in the value of y **could** be explained by variations in the value of x.

Note. We do not conclude that 81% of variations in y are caused by variations in x. We say that 81% of variations in y can be explained by variations in x.

Cause and effect

relationship exists between two variables when a change in one causes the change in the other.

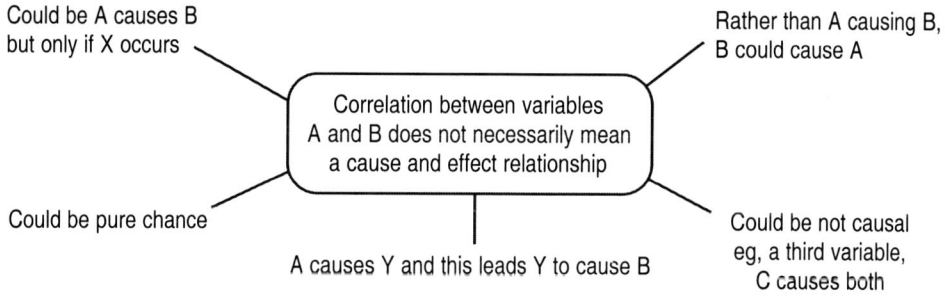

However, if there is a cause and effect relationship, there must be correlation.

| Data and information | Data analysis considerations | **Spreadsheets** | Charts | Big data and data analytics | Protection of commercially sensitive information |

Spreadsheets

Common uses in finance

- Accounting records
- Budgets and forecasts
- What if analysis/scenario analysis

Risks from spreadsheet use

- Errors
- Lack of consistency in design
- Poor design
- Loss of data

Principles of good spreadsheet practice

- Adopt standards (eg, over cell formats)
- Identify the audience
- 'About' sheet to document spreadsheet
- Design for longevity
- Clearly identify inputs, workings and outputs
- Avoid advanced features when simpler ones can do
- Backup and version control
- Protect

Basic spreadsheet functions

Sum

Adds the values in a range of cells

=**SUM(cell range)** where the sum range is the range of cells to be added.

Average

Used to calculate the arithmetic mean for a set of values

=**AVERAGE(number 1, number 2)** where each number is an actual number, a cell reference or range of cells that contain numbers.

Countif

Counts the number of cells in a range that contain specific content

=**COUNTIF(range, criteria)** where the range is the range of cells being examined and criteria being the content being looked for.

| Data and information | Data analysis considerations | Spreadsheets | **Charts** | Big data and data analytics | Protection of commercially sensitive information |

Bar charts

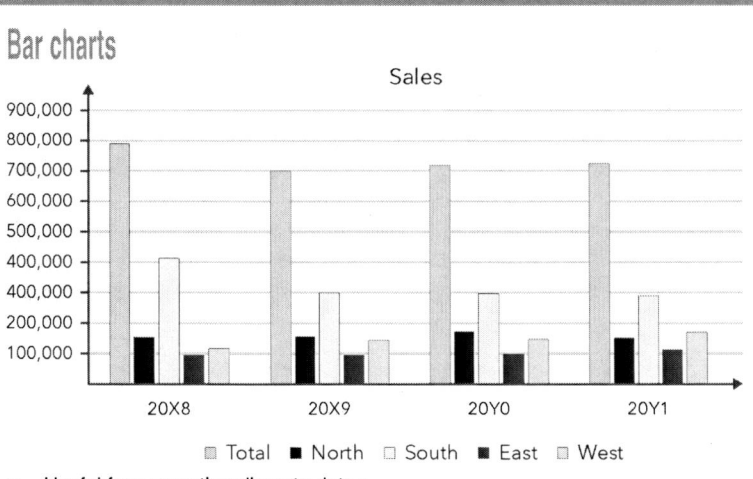

- Useful for presenting discrete data
- Useful for comparisons between data sets (eg, sales by region)

Pie charts

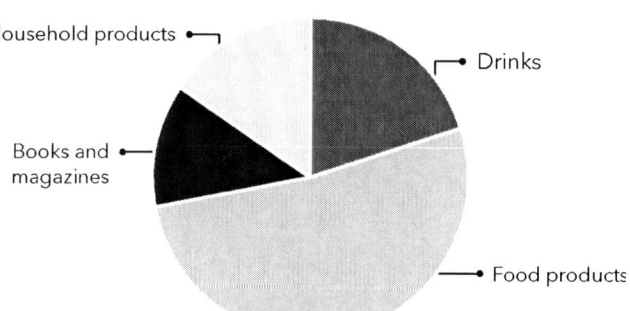

- Useful for showing components that make up a total
- Not useful for more than one period

| Data and information | Data analysis considerations | Spreadsheets | **Charts** | Big data and data analytics | Protection of commercially sensitive information |

Line charts

Quarterly sales and profits

- Useful for presenting long term trends
- Several data series can be presented in one chart

| Data and information | Data analysis considerations | Spreadsheets | Charts | **Big data and data analytics** | Protection of commercially sensitive information |

Big data

Datasets whose size is beyond the ability of typical database software to capture, store, manage and analyse.

Characteristics of big data

- Volume
- Velocity
- Variety
- Veracity

Risks of big data and data analytics

- Storage
- Workforce skills
- Data dependency
- Information overload
- Data privacy
- Data security

Data analytics

Data analytics is the process of collecting, organising and analysing large sets of data to discover patterns and other information which an organisation can use for its future business decisions. It is not only concerned with the tools and methods to obtain, manage and analyse data; it is also about extracting value from data and translating it from asset to product.

| Data and information | Data analysis considerations | Spreadsheets | Charts | **Big data and data analytics** | Protection of commercially sensitive information |

Data analytics

The following table describes **four types of data analytics**, each of which seeks to answer a different question.

Type of data analytics	Question to be answered
Descriptive analytics	**What has happened?**
	For example, determining whether sales of a product increased or decreased following a price change.
Diagnostic analytics	**Why has something happened?**
	For example, analysing why the price change resulted in more or fewer people buying the product.
Predictive analytics	**What is likely to happen in the future?**
	For example, forecasting what could happen to sales if the price of the product is increased next year.
Prescriptive analytics	**What is the best course of action?**
	For example, determining a future pricing strategy for the product.

| Data and information | Data analysis considerations | Spreadsheets | Charts | Big data and data analytics | **Protection of commercially sensitive information** |

Protection of commercially sensitive information

Data protection laws, such as the **Data Protection Act 2018** are designed to protect data held about private individuals and do not extend to commercial data such as trade secrets, business strategy and financial information.

Intellectual property (IP)

Intellectual property (IP) is a form of intangible asset that a company creates through the application of the skill and knowledge of its employees.

Examples of IP	Methods of IP protection
<ul><li>The names of products or brands</li><li>Inventions</li><li>The design or look of products</li><li>Items that the company wrote, made or produced</li></ul>	<ul><li>Copyright</li><li>Design right</li><li>Trademark</li><li>Registered design</li><li>Patent</li></ul>

| Data and information | Data analysis considerations | Spreadsheets | Charts | Big data and data analytics | **Protection of commercially sensitive information** |

A key threat to commercially sensitive information is from those who have access to the information through their employment. There is a risk that the information could be **accidentally** or **deliberately leaked** by an **employee**.

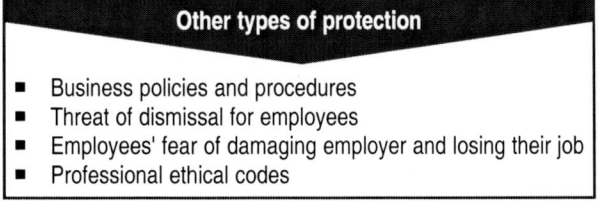

Other types of protection

- Business policies and procedures
- Threat of dismissal for employees
- Employees' fear of damaging employer and losing their job
- Professional ethical codes

2: Technology, ethics and sustainability

Topic List

Developments in technology

Business and the accountancy profession

Problems with data

Ethics and professional scepticism

Sustainability

This chapter examines some recent developments in technology and how they impact on the accountancy profession. It also looks at the ethical issues relating to data and information, including data bias and professional scepticism.

| Developments in technology | Business and the accountancy profession | Problems with data | Ethics and professional scepticism | Sustainability |

Distributed ledger technology (DLT)

encompasses a range of decentralised database systems where transactions are recorded and validated across multiple sites.

Blockchain

is a specific form of DLT that records data in a decentralised and immutable manner across multiple nodes. It ensures the data cannot be altered after the fact.

Digital assets

is any text or media file that is formatted into a binary source and that includes the right to use it; digital files that do not carry this right are not considered digital assets.

Fintech

the use of technology to improve and automate financial services.

Machine learning

is the ability of a computational device to learn from large volumes of training data and improve upon a given task without having been explicitly programmed to do so.

Cryptocurrency

a digital asset that is designed to function as a medium of exchange and store of value.

| Developments in technology | Business and the accountancy profession | Problems with data | Ethics and professional scepticism | Sustainability |

Artificial intelligence (AI)

is the field of study and application involving the creation and use of advanced computer systems to perform tasks traditionally requiring human intelligence.

Computer vision	AI focussing on identifying information from images and video
Generative	AI that creates text and images in response to human prompts (eg, ChatGPT, Copilot)
Natural language processing	AI that allows understanding and manipulation of human language (eg, Apple's Siri, Amazon's Alexa)

Automation

The development and implementation of technology to oversee and manage the production and distribution of goods and services.

Robotic process automation (RPA)

A software solution that replicates a business process, designed to do a task that would otherwise be performed manually.

| Developments in technology | **Business and the accountancy profession** | Problems with data | Ethics and professional scepticism | Sustainability |

Impacts of technology on business

Developments in information technology affect and disrupt all areas of business. This disruption is a consequence of the developments being both rapid in pace and wide and deep in their scope.

Impact	Impact on business
New sources of data and information	Big data and data analytics can help an organisation to improve its understanding of its customers.
System-generated data	Data analytics can be run on data contained in an organisation's internal systems (such as operations and finance) for performance measurement purposes and to help identify operational inefficiencies.
Virtual supply chains	Technological links between the organisation and its supply chain enables large and complex supply chains to be formed through the sharing of knowledge and other forms of collaboration that enable components and products to be made in the most cost-effective manner.
Opportunities for new products	Technology has allowed the development of new products and services that were not previously possible. Apps are a relatively simple way to create a new product or service and sell it globally for a relatively low cost.
Removal of barriers to entry into markets	As well as providing opportunities to create new products and services, technology has helped remove barriers to entry (such as cost) in some markets to enable more organisations to enter markets that they could not enter previously.

Impacts of technology on the accountancy profession

The following two tables show how technology has impacted both accountants and auditors.

Technology development	Impact on accounting
Automation, machine learning and artificial intelligence	Maintaining ledgers and preparing reconciliations is no longer performed by humans.
More powerful systems	Processing speeds increase freeing up the accountant to perform value-adding roles.
System innovations and applications	Accountants required to provide advice on the adoption of innovations and how to use and account for them.
Digital contracts and transactions	Accountants are involved in new ways of recording transactions.
New types of data, information and risks	Increased need for sound judgement in accountants.
New types of goods and services	Accountants to advise clients and employers on how to account for items arising from new technology such as digital assets.
Transparency in recording and sharing data	Distributed ledgers, for instance, mean there is more clarity about resources due to the improved recording of transactions.

Technology development	Impact on auditing
Audit analytics and intelligent systems	New systems allow complete checks on data and allow 100% of transactions to be audited automatically on a continuous basis.
Smart contracts	The audit of smart contracts to take place as the smart contract is being created, before transactions under it occur.
Data analytics	Predictive analytics helps to target risk and improves the relevance of audits.
Software controls and data sets	Audit work to focus on validating controls within the accounting software and on interpreting complex data sets.
Innovations such as distributed ledger technology and advanced accounting systems	Properly functioning distributed ledgers and software reduce the need for auditors to audit transactions and verify the ownership of assets.
Regulation	Audit regulations must adapt to technological developments.

| Developments in technology | **Business and the accountancy profession** | Problems with data | Ethics and professional scepticism | Sustainability |

| Developments in technology | Business and the accountancy profession | **Problems with data** | Ethics and professional scepticism | Sustainability |

Definitions	
Obsolescence risk	The risk that investments in technology quickly become obsolescent
Inexplicability risk	The risk that humans do not understand the algorithms developed by the machine in ML
Data protection issues	Companies should only hold personal data for specified purposes, and should not be held for longer than required
Automation risk	This relates to whether or not businesses have the right staff with the skills to work in a more automated environment
Data bias	When data is not representative of the population that is being analysed
Graphical data issues	For example, manipulating axes on a graph or bar chart or omitting some data
AI risks	For example, confidentiality risk, responsibility for mistakes, ethical decisions

| Developments in technology | Business and the accountancy profession | **Problems with data** | Ethics and professional scepticism | Sustainability |

Data is biased when it is not representative of the population. This can occur:

- during data collection (eg, some members having a lower chance of being included); and
- in analysis or conclusions (eg, people can introduce bias).

Bias can occur in charts and infographics by:

- manipulating axes on a graph or chart; or
- omitting some data.

Bias can occur in AI algorithms as a result of:

- training the algorithm on data not sufficiently diverse; and
- humans creating rules with implicit biases.

Professional scepticism must be applied when dealing with data.

Bias	Meaning
Selection	This occurs when the data is not selected randomly and leads to a sample that is not representative of the population.
Self-selection	This occurs when individuals select themselves. Those who choose to respond may have a certain characteristic or interest that leads them to respond.
Observer	This occurs when observing and recording results and relates to interpretation. The researcher allows their assumptions (which may be unconscious) to influence their observations.
Omitted variable	This occurs when a variable is excluded from the data model and therefore the cause of a change in one variable is incorrectly attributed to another variable in the model.
Cognitive	This relates to human perception and includes bias depending on how data is presented (eg, infographics or the order of presentation) and 'anchoring' (eg, being influenced or 'stuck' on last year's numbers).
Confirmation	This occurs when people see data that confirms their beliefs and they ignore (consciously or sub-consciously) data that disagrees with their beliefs.
Survivorship	This is the tendency towards studying successful outcomes while excluding unsuccessful outcomes. An example of this is the exclusion of failed companies in business performance studies because they no longer exist.

| Developments in technology | Business and the accountancy profession | Problems with data | **Ethics and professional scepticism** | Sustainability |

ICAEW fundamental principles

Integrity	Members must be straightforward and professional in all business relationships.
Objectivity	Members should avoid all bias, prejudice and partiality.
Professional competence and due care	Members must not perform roles which they cannot do without reasonable care, competence and diligence. They must stay technically up to date and comply with professional standards.
Confidentiality	Members should not disclose confidential information without permission or legal or professional right or duty.
Professional behaviour	Members should protect their reputation and that of the professional body.

Professional scepticism

means assessing information, estimates and explanations critically, with a questioning mind, and being alert to possible misstatements due to error or fraud.

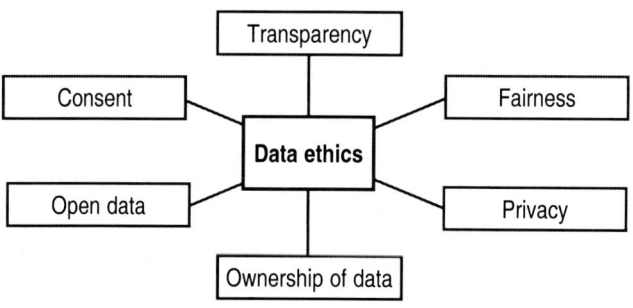

| Developments in technology | Business and the accountancy profession | Problems with data | Ethics and professional scepticism | **Sustainability** |

Sustainability

The ability to 'meet the needs of the present without compromising the ability of future generations to meet their own needs' (Brundtland Report, 1987).

Sustainable development

The process by which we achieve sustainability.

Corporate responsibility

The actions, activities and obligations of business in achieving sustainability.

Governance

The way organisations are directed and controlled by senior officers.

ESG

Environmental, social and governance (ESG) approaches sustainability through a corporate lens considering risks on business and enterprise values.

A healthy environment underpins a healthy society which underpins a healthy economy.

United Nations Sustainability Development Goals (SDGs)

SDGs wedding cake image

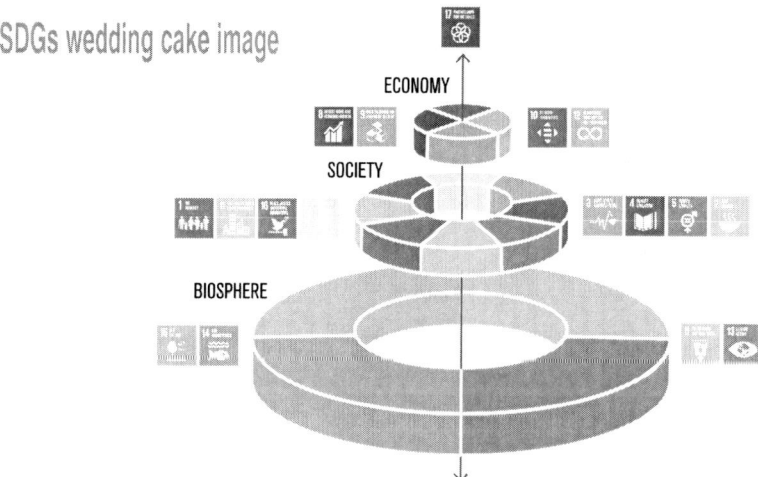

| Developments in technology | Business and the accountancy profession | Problems with data | Ethics and professional scepticism | **Sustainability** |

Impacts

How the decisions an organisation makes affect environmental, societal and governance issues. 'Inward-out' approach.

Dependencies

How the current and future environmental, social and governance issues can affect the organisation's ability to create and maintain value. 'Outward-in' approach.

Double materiality

Considering not only the sustainability issues that might create financial risks for the company (financial materiality), but also those sustainability issues where a company's activities materially impact on people and the environment (impact materiality).

Examples of impacts	**Examples of dependencies**
- Worker rights - Human rights - Health and safety policy - Waste - Greenhouse gas emissions - Water usage - Land usage - Biodiversity	- Worker health - Workplace diversity - Climatic conditions - Resource availability - Regulation - Consumer expectations - Other stakeholder expectations - Risks to organisational reputation

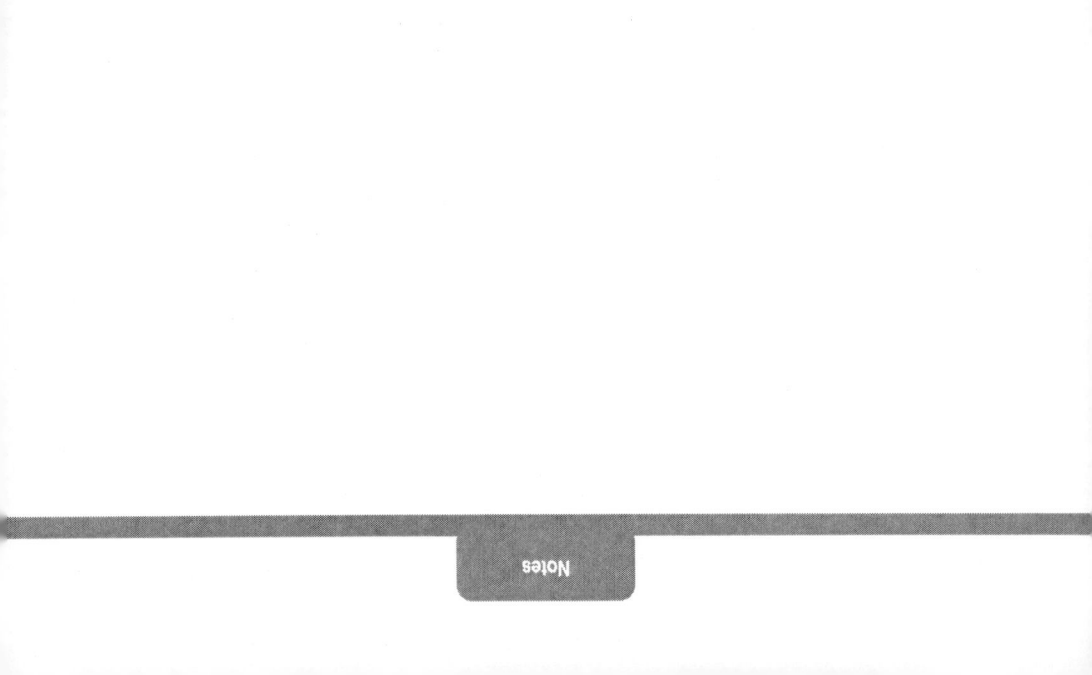

3: The fundamentals of costing

Topic List

What is cost accounting?

Basic cost concepts

Cost classification – inventory

Cost classification – planning

Cost classification – control

The classification of costs is an essential management accounting technique. The aim of the cost accounting system is to provide information to do the following:

- *Calculate the cost of a product or service*
- *Compare actual costs to budgeted costs*
- *Work out prices for contracts*

Make sure you are familiar with the terms used here for the different types of cost. These appear later in the syllabus when we look at unit costs.

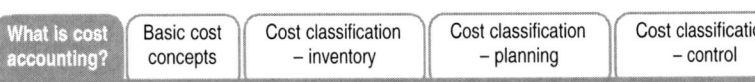

| What is cost accounting? | Basic cost concepts | Cost classification – inventory | Cost classification – planning | Cost classification – control |

Managing involves

- Planning
- Controlling
- Decision making

Cost accounting provides information to

- Establish inventory valuations (Chapter 4)
- Plan (Chapter 8)
- Control (Chapter 10)
- Make decisions (Chapter 7)

The management accountant

Provides the manager with:

- Assistance in planning
- Assistance in controlling
- Assistance in decision making

(Note that IAS 1 changes the titles of financial statements as they will be used in IFRSs.

1 'Balance sheet' will become 'statement of financial position'

2 'Income statement' will become 'statement of profit or loss'

3 'Cash flow statement' will become 'statement of cash flows'

Entities are not required to use the new titles in their financial statements. Consequently these passcards may use these terms interchangeably.)

> The data used to prepare financial accounts and management accounts are the same. The differences between these accounts arise because the data is analysed differently.

Financial accounts

- Prepared for external individuals
- Detail performance of a defined period
- Legal requirements for limited companies to prepare FA
- Format of published FA determined by
  - Law (eg, Companies Acts)
  - FRSs
  - IASs
- FA cover business as a whole
- FA information monetary (mostly)
- Historic picture of past operations

Management accounts

- Prepared for internal managers of an organisation
- Aid management in recording, planning and controlling organisation's activities
- Help decision-making process
- No legal requirements to prepare MA
- Format of MA at discretion of management
- MA can focus on specific areas of an organisation's activities
- MA incorporate non-monetary measures
- Historic record and future planning tool

What is cost accounting?	**Basic cost concepts**	Cost classification – inventory	Cost classification – planning	Cost classification – control

Cost unit

is the basic measure of a product or service for which costs are determined.

Example

- Patient episode (in a hospital)
- Barrel (in the brewing industry)
- Room (in a hotel)

Cost object

is anything for which we are trying to ascertain the cost.

Example

- The cost of a product
- The cost of a service
- The cost of operating a department

Composite cost unit

is a cost made up of two parts, for example patient/day cost.

| What is cost accounting? | Basic cost concepts | **Cost classification – inventory** | Cost classification – planning | Cost classification – control |

Direct cost

is a cost that can be **traced in full** to the cost unit.

Direct costs include

- Direct materials
- Direct labour
- Direct expenses
- Total direct costs = prime cost

Indirect cost (overhead)

is a cost that is incurred whilst making a product but which **cannot be traced directly** to the cost unit.

Indirect costs include

- Indirect materials ⎫
- Indirect labour   ⎬ = Production overhead
- Indirect expenses ⎭
- Administration overhead
- Selling and distribution overhead

Total product cost

Product cost → identified with product   Period cost → deducted as expense

What is cost accounting?	Basic cost concepts	Cost classification – inventory	**Cost classification – planning**	Cost classification – control

Fixed cost

is a cost which is unaffected by changes in the level of activity within a relevant range.

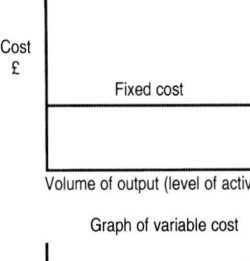

Graph of fixed cost

Cost £

Fixed cost

Volume of output (level of activity)

Example

- Rent of a building
- Business rates
- Salary of a director

Variable cost

is a cost which tends to vary with the level of activity. The variable cost per unit is the same for **each unit** produced.

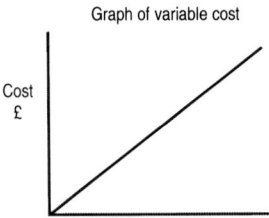

Graph of variable cost

Cost £

Volume of output (level of activity)

Example

- Direct materials
- Direct labour
- Sales commission (varies with volume of sales)

Semi-variable/semi-fixed/ mixed cost

are costs that are part-fixed and part-variable and are therefore partly affected by changes in the level of activity.

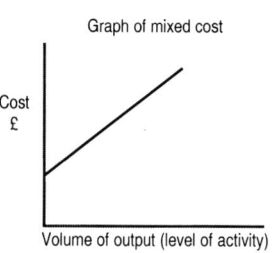

Graph of mixed cost

Example

- Telephone bills
- Sales person's salary

Relevant range and stepped costs

are fixed in nature but only within certain levels of activity.

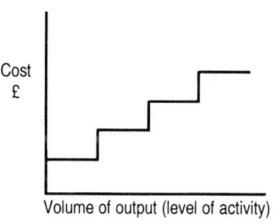

Example

- Supervisors' salary costs
- Royalties

| What is cost accounting? | Basic cost concepts | Cost classification – inventory | Cost classification – planning | **Cost classification – control** |

Responsibility accounting

segregates revenues and costs into areas of personal responsibility to monitor and assess performance of each part of an organisation.

Responsibility centre

is a department or organisational function whose performance is the direct responsibility of a specific manager.

Controllable costs

can be influenced by management decisions and actions.

Uncontrollable costs

cannot be affected by management within a given time span.

4: Calculating unit costs (Part 1)

Topic List

Direct and indirect costs

Inventory valuation

The management information system provides information on unit costs as the basis for management planning and control.

Inventory valuation is used to value materials for management accounts and for financial reporting purposes.

Direct and indirect costs	Inventory valuation

Direct material cost

is all material becoming part of the cost unit. It forms part of the **prime cost**.

Direct expenses

any other costs (other than direct material cost and direct wages) incurred on a specific cost unit. They are part of the **prime cost**.

Direct labour costs

are all wages paid for labour. They form part of the **prime cost**.

Indirect cost (overhead)

is a cost that is incurred whilst making a product but which **cannot be traced directly** to the product, service or department.

Direct and indirect costs | **Inventory valuation**

We will use the following information about receipts and issues of materials in the remainder of this chapter.

Date	Receipts Quantity Units	Receipts Value £	Issues Quantity Units	Issues Value £	Balance Quantity Units	Balance Value £
March 1					10	100
March 10	30	450				
March 12			25			
March 20	20	320				
March 23			15			

4: Calculating unit costs (Part 1)

	Direct and indirect costs	Inventory valuation

FIFO

FIFO assumes that materials are issued out of inventory in the order in which they were delivered into inventory.

Example - FIFO

	£
March 12 issue = (10 □ £10) + (15 □ £15) =	325
March 23 issue = 15 □ £15	225
Closing inventory = 20 □ £16	320
	870

FIFO is an historical cost method.

Advantages ☑ and disadvantages ☒

- ☑ Logical, represents what is physically happening
- ☑ Easy to understand and explain
- ☑ Inventory valuation based on replacement cost
- ☒ Cumbersome to operate
- ☒ Cost comparison and decision making difficult due to price variations
- ☒ Issue prices can lag behind market value if inflation is high

LIFO

LIFO assumes that materials are issued out of inventory in the reverse order to which they were delivered.

Example - LIFO

	£
March 12 issue = 25 × £15	375
March 23 issue = 15 × £16	240
Closing inventory = (5 × £16) + (5 × £15)	
+ (10 × £10)	255
	870

Material issues are based on market value.

Advantages ☑ and disadvantages ☒

- ☑ Issues are at close to market value
- ☑ Current costs used in decisions
- ☒ Cumbersome to operate
- ☒ Opposite to what is physically happening
- ☒ Difficult to explain
- ☒ Decision making can be difficult due to price variations

Direct and indirect costs	Inventory valuation

Cumulative weighted average (AVCO)

involves calculating a weighted average price by dividing total cost by total number of units in inventory. A new average price is calculated when a new receipt of material occurs.

Example

	£
March 12 issue at £(100 + 450)/40	
= £13.75 × 25	343.75
March 23 issue at £((13.75 × 15) + 320)/35	
= £15.04 × 15	225.60
Closing inventory = 20 × £15.04	300.80
	870.15

(The 15p is a rounding difference.)

Advantages ☑ and disadvantages ☒

- ☑ Price fluctuations are smoothed out so decision making is easier
- ☑ Easier to administer than FIFO and LIFO
- ☒ Resulting price rarely an actual price
- ☒ Prices lag a little behind market values if there is gradual inflation

Periodic weighted average pricing

is an average method where a single average is calculated at the end of the period based on all purchases for the period.

$$\text{Periodic weighted average price} = \frac{\text{Cost of opening inventory} + \text{Total cost of receipts in period}}{\text{Units in opening inventory} + \text{Total units received in period}}$$

Unless stated to the contrary, assume the cumulative average method (rather than the periodic average method) is required in an exam question.

| Direct and indirect costs | Inventory valuation |

FIFO, LIFO and cumulative weighted average inventory valuation methods produce different costs of sales and hence profits

Opening inventory values and purchase costs are the same for each method

Therefore different costs of sales are due to different closing inventory valuations

Profit differences = differences in closing inventory valuations

5: Calculating unit costs (Part 2)

Topic List

Absorption costing (AC)

Costing methods

Management need to know the full cost of items for certain decisions. These decisions include determining selling prices and valuing finished goods inventory.

Absorption costing is a method for sharing indirect costs between cost units.

*Absorption costing treats fixed production overheads as **product costs** which are then added to the cost of inventory.*

| | Absorption costing (AC) | Costing methods |

Allocation

is the process by which whole cost items are charged directly to a cost unit or cost centre.

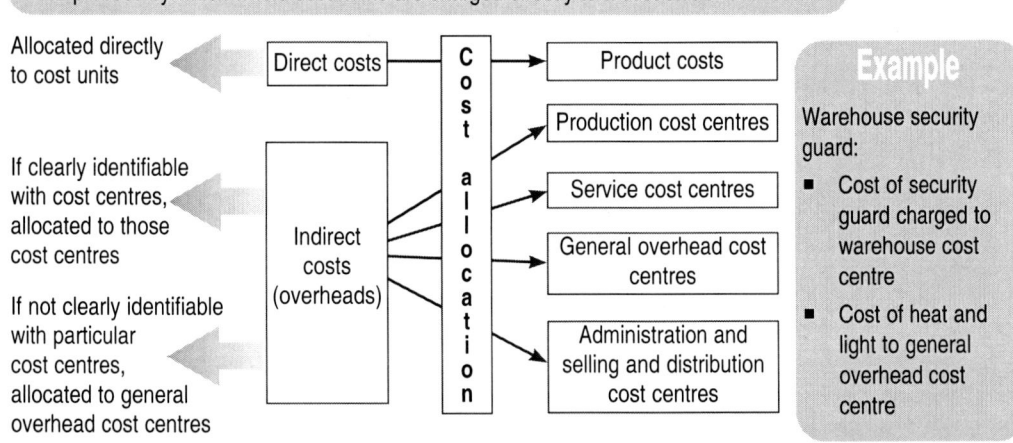

Allocated directly to cost units

If clearly identifiable with cost centres, allocated to those cost centres

If not clearly identifiable with particular cost centres, allocated to general overhead cost centres

Direct costs

Indirect costs (overheads)

Cost allocation

Product costs

Production cost centres

Service cost centres

General overhead cost centres

Administration and selling and distribution cost centres

Example

Warehouse security guard:

- Cost of security guard charged to warehouse cost centre
- Cost of heat and light to general overhead cost centre

Apportionment

The first stage of overhead apportionment is the identification of all overheads as production, service, administration or selling and distribution.

Overheads within general overhead cost centres
- Share out between other cost centres
- Use a fair basis of apportionment

The second stage of overhead apportionment is to apportion the costs of service cost centres (both directly allocated and apportioned) to production cost centres. This is known as reapportionment.

Method
- Apportion costs for service cost centre with largest costs first
- Then other service cost centres are apportioned between production cost centres

	Absorption costing (AC)	Costing methods

The final stage in absorption costing is the absorption of overheads into product costs using overhead absorption rates (OARs).

Bases of absorption

- Per unit (identical units)
- Per direct labour hour (labour intensive)
- Per machine hour (machine intensive)

Departmental OARs

- Used instead of blanket (single factory) OARs
- Reflect different times spent by different products in production cost centres

Predetermined OARs

Many overheads are not known until the end of a period. Waiting until the end of the period would cause delays in invoicing, inventory valuations and so on. Random fluctuations in overheads would create variable OARs from month to month.

$$\frac{\text{Budgeted overheads allocated and apportioned to production cost centres}}{\text{Budgeted activity levels (hours, units etc) on which rate to be based}}$$

Over-/under-absorbed overheads

These arise because the OAR is predetermined from budget estimates. When actual overheads incurred and overheads absorbed using predetermined OARs differ, there will be an over or under absorption of overheads.

Reasons

- Actual OH ☐ budgeted OH
- Actual activity level ☐ budgeted activity level
- 1 and 2 above (together)

Accounting for over/under absorption of overheads

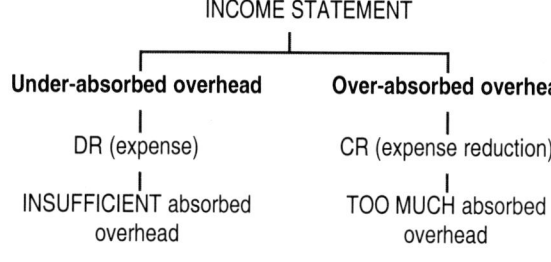

	Absorption costing (AC)	Costing methods

A job

is a cost unit which consists of a single order or contract.

Profit on jobs

Profit may be expressed either as a percentage of **job cost** (such as 15%) (25/100) mark-up or as a percentage **of price**, such as 20% (25/125) margin.

Batch costing

is very similar to job costing.

$$\text{Cost per unit} = \frac{\text{Total batch cost}}{\text{No. units in batch}}$$

Features of job costing

- Work is undertaken to customers' special requirements.
- Each order is of short duration.
- Jobs move through operations as a continuously identifiable unit.
- Jobs are usually individual and separate records should be maintained.

Job costs are collected on a job cost sheet/card.

Contract costing

is a method of **job costing** where the work undertaken is bespoke and costs involved are significant. A formal contract is made between the customer and supplier.

Features of contract costing

- **Formal contract** between supplier and customer
- Work is undertaken to **customer's special requirements**
- Work is for a **relatively long duration**
- Work is frequently **constructional** in nature
- The **costing method** is similar to **job costing**
- The work is frequently **based on site**

Overhead costs

are added **periodically** based on predetermined OAR.

Contract accounts

are job or WIP accounts recording the direct costs and overheads charged to the contract.

| | Absorption costing (AC) | Costing methods |

Process costing

is used where it is not possible to identify separate units of production so costs are averaged. Typical process costing uses are in oil refining, food and drink and soap manufacture.

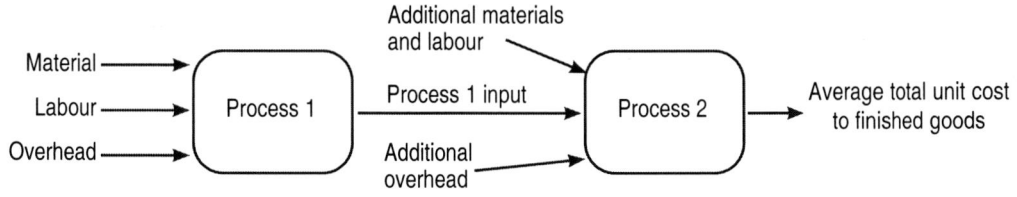

Process costing can also be applied in a service environment. For example, in an organisation that provides a shirt laundering service the processes involved might be as follows:

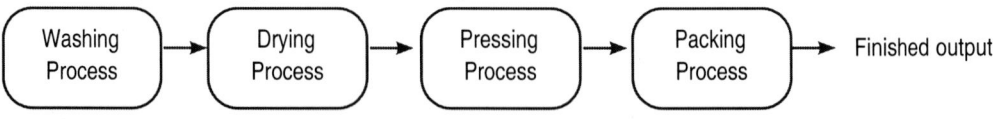

6: Marginal costing and absorption costing

Topic List

Marginal costing (MC)

MC and AC compared

*Marginal costing treats all fixed costs as **period costs** so that these are excluded from the costs used in valuing inventory. This approach means that marginal costing and absorption costing produce different inventory valuations. Therefore profit figures will also be different under the two systems.*

	Marginal costing (MC)	MC and AC compared

Marginal cost

is the cost of one unit of product/service which would be avoided if that unit were not produced/provided = variable cost.

Contribution

equals (sales revenue – variable (marginal) cost of sales). It is short for contribution towards covering fixed overheads and making a profit.

Marginal costing

- Only variable costs charged as cost of sales.
- Closing inventories are valued at marginal cost.
- Fixed costs are treated as period costs.
- Period costs are charged in full to the income statement.
- If sales increase by one item, profit will increase by contribution for one item.
- Contribution per unit is constant at all levels of output and sales.

Marginal costing (MC)	**MC and AC compared**

> The difference in reported profits is calculated as the difference between the fixed production overhead included in the opening and closing inventory valuations using absorption costing.

MARGINAL COSTING → Closing inventories are valued at marginal production cost

ABSORPTION COSTING → Closing inventories are valued at full production cost

RECONCILIATION

	£
Marginal costing profit	X
Adjust for fixed overheads in inventory:	
+ increase / – decrease	X/(X)
Absorption costing profit	X

Inventory levels

Increase in a period
- Absorption costing reports higher profit
- Fixed overheads included in closing inventory
- Cost of sales decreased
- Hence, profit higher

Decrease in a period
- Absorption costing reports lower profit
- Fixed overheads included in opening inventory
- Cost of sales increased
- Hence, profit lower

| Marginal costing (MC) | MC and AC compared |

Arguments in favour of absorption costing

- ☑ Fixed production costs are incurred in order to make output and so it is only 'fair' to charge all output with a share of these costs.
- ☑ Closing inventory will be valued in accordance with accounting standards.
- ☑ Appraising products in terms of contribution gives no indication of whether fixed costs are being covered.

Arguments in favour of marginal costing

- ☑ It is simple to operate.
- ☑ There are no arbitrary fixed cost apportionments.
- ☑ Fixed costs in a period will be the same regardless of the level of output and so it makes sense to charge them in full as a cost of the period.
- ☑ It is realistic to value closing inventory items at the (directly attributable) cost to produce an extra unit.
- ☑ It focuses on variable costs which are most likely to change as a result of a decision.

7: Pricing calculations

Topic List

Full cost-plus pricing

Marginal cost-plus pricing

Mark-ups and margins

Demand and supply

Transfer pricing

The calculation of a selling price for goods or services is an important management decision.

Ideally, a selling price will cover costs and still encourage customers to buy.

Organisations often transfer goods and services internally. Transfer prices cover these transfers and give signals to management to encourage optimal decision-making.

| Full cost-plus pricing | Marginal cost-plus pricing | Mark-ups and margins | Demand and supply | Transfer pricing |

In practice, cost is one of the most important influences on price.

- Full cost-plus
- Marginal cost-plus

Full cost-plus pricing

is a method of determining the sales price by calculating the full cost of the product and adding a percentage **mark-up** for profit.

Example

Variable cost of production (product A)
= £4 per unit
Fixed cost of production (product A)
= £3 per unit
Price is to be 40% higher than full cost

Full cost per unit = £(4 + 3) = £7

Price = £7 □ $\frac{140\%}{100}$

= £9.80

Advantages

☑ Quick, simple, cheap method
☑ Ensures company covers fixed costs

Disadvantages

☒ Does not recognise profit-maximising combination of price and demand
☒ Budgeted output needs to be established
☒ Suitable basis for overhead absorption needed

| Full cost-plus pricing | **Marginal cost-plus pricing** | Mark-ups and margins | Demand and supply | Transfer pricing |

Marginal cost-plus pricing

is a method of determining the sales price by adding a profit margin onto either marginal cost of production or marginal cost of sales.

Example

Direct materials (product B) = £15
Direct labour (product B) = £3
Variable overhead (product B) = £7
Price of product B = £40

Profit = £40 − £(15 + 3 + 7) = £15

Profit margin = $\dfrac{£15}{£25} \times 100\% = 60\%$

Advantages

- ☑ Simple and easy method
- ☑ Mark-up percentage can be varied
- ☑ Draws management attention to contribution

Disadvantages

- ☒ Does not ensure that attention paid to demand conditions, competitors' prices and profit maximisation
- ☒ Ignores fixed overheads – so must make sure sales price high enough to make profit

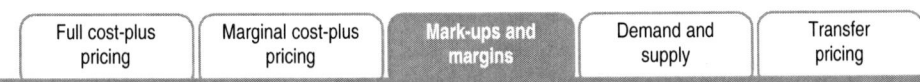

| Full cost-plus pricing | Marginal cost-plus pricing | **Mark-ups and margins** | Demand and supply | Transfer pricing |

Full cost-plus pricing

Sales price = full cost of the product + % mark-up for profit

Marginal cost-plus pricing/mark-up pricing

Sales price = marginal cost of production (or marginal cost of sales) + % mark-up for profit

Margins and mark-ups

With a cost/profit/sales structure of:

	%
Cost	80
Profit	20
Sales	100

Profit may be expressed as:

- A % of **cost of sales** eg, 25% (20/80) **mark-up**
- A % of **sales** eg, 20% (20/100) **margin**

Examples

If the full cost of product X is £200 and a 25% **return on sales** is required, selling price = £200/0.75 = £266.67.

Investment in product Z is £1,000,000 pa and a return of 20% is required. If a unit of Z costs £100 and 20,000 units will be sold, the selling price based on this **target return on investment** is:

$$= \frac{\text{expected revenue (= required return + expected cost)}}{\text{units}}$$

$$= ((£1,000,000 \times 20\%) + (£100 \times 20,000)) / 20,000 = £110$$

If product K sells for £60 and the mark-up is 20%, the cost of K = £60/1.2 = £50

If Product B costs £100, a selling price based on a margin of 25% = £100/0.75 = £133.33

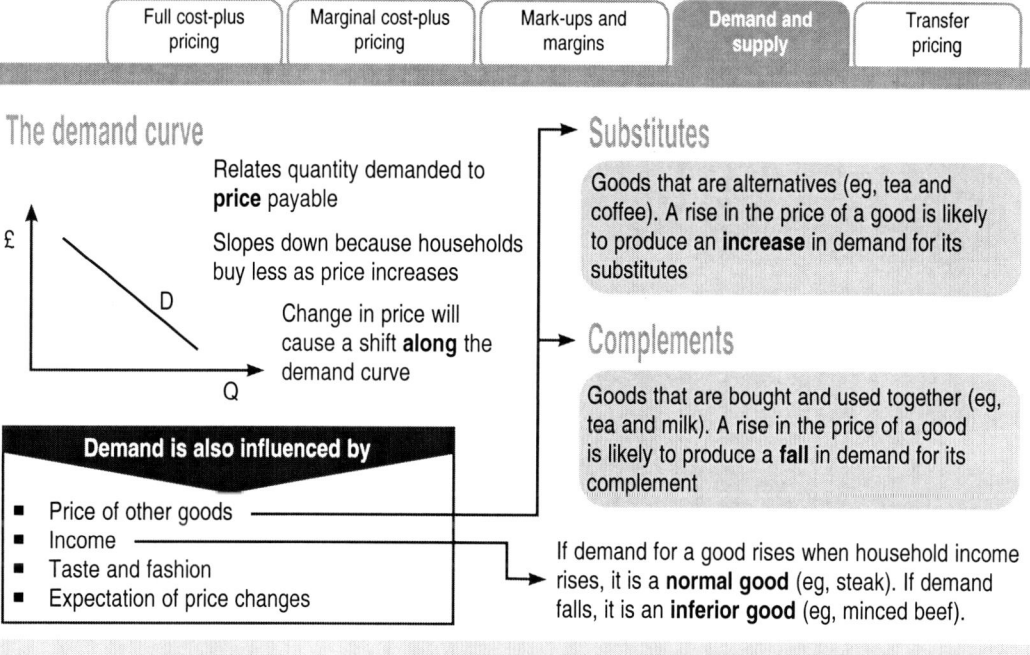

| Full cost-plus pricing | Marginal cost-plus pricing | Mark-ups and margins | **Demand and supply** | Transfer pricing |

Remember! The demand curve shows how demand responds to a change in price and nothing else! Any change in the other factors that affect demand cause a shift in the position of the demand curve.

A leftward shift may be caused by

- A fall in household income
- A fall in the price of substitutes
- A rise in the price of complements
- A change in taste away from the good
- An expected fall in price

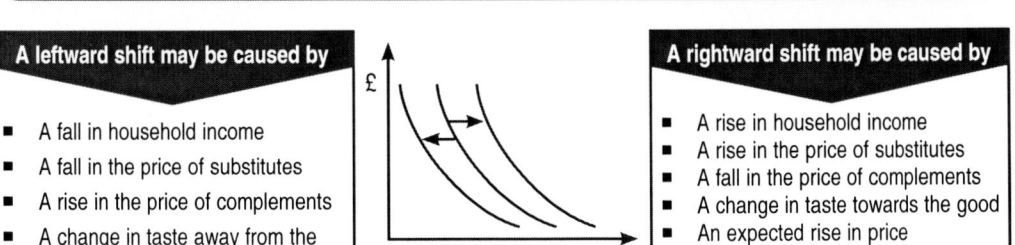

A rightward shift may be caused by

- A rise in household income
- A rise in the price of substitutes
- A fall in the price of complements
- A change in taste towards the good
- An expected rise in price

An expectation of a fall in price will lead consumers to put off their purchases in the hope of benefiting from the lower price later. An expected price rise will lead consumers to buy early and stockpile in order to avoid paying a higher price later.

The supply curve

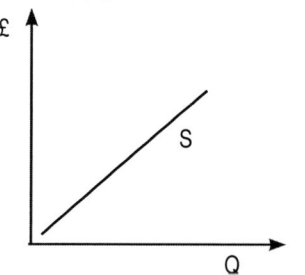

Relates quantity supplied to **price** payable

Slopes up because firms want to supply more if they can get a higher price

Change in price will cause a shift **along** the supply curve

Supply is also influenced by:

- Price of other goods
- Price of goods in joint supply
- Costs of making the item
- Changes in technology

Changes in these factors will cause a shift of the supply curve.

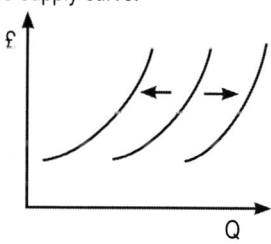

| Full cost-plus pricing | Marginal cost-plus pricing | Mark-ups and margins | Demand and supply | Transfer pricing |

The market mechanism

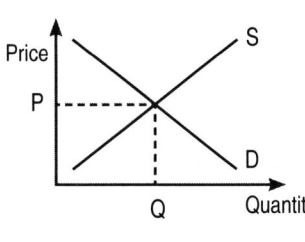

The market mechanism brings supply and demand together at the **equilibrium price** P. This is also the **market clearing price** since quantity Q is both offered and demanded and there is neither surplus nor shortage.

Functions of the market mechanism

- Market prices and their movements act as **signals** to producers, enabling them to produce what is most needed.

- When a firm operates efficiently, responding to market signals and controlling its costs, it receives a **reward** in the form of profit.

- The actions of firms in responding to the profit opportunities **allocate** resources to their best use.

Consumer surplus: some would have paid more than the market price

Producer surplus: some would have sold at less than the market price

A shift of the demand or supply curve causes:
- A rise or fall in market price P
- An increase or decrease in quantity supplied Q

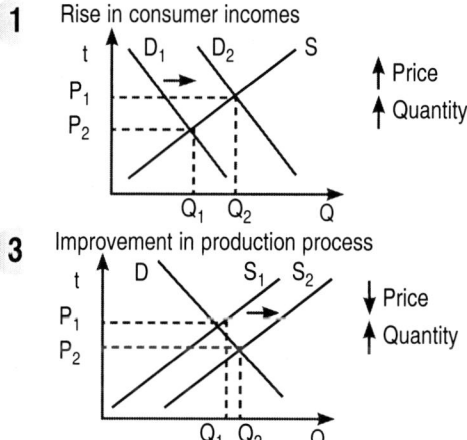

1 Rise in consumer incomes
↑ Price
↑ Quantity

3 Improvement in production process
↓ Price
↑ Quantity

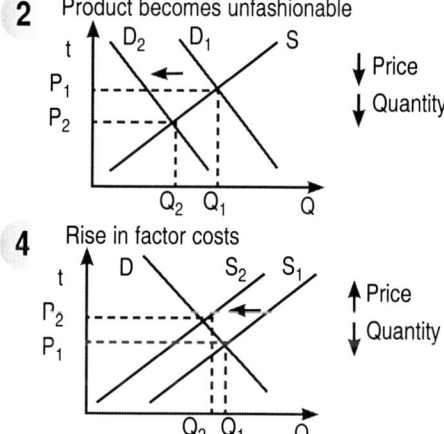

2 Product becomes unfashionable
↓ Price
↓ Quantity

4 Rise in factor costs
↑ Price
↓ Quantity

| Full cost-plus pricing | Marginal cost-plus pricing | Mark-ups and margins | **Demand and supply** | Transfer pricing |

Upward sloping demand curve

- Giffen goods – basic goods where a rise in price means the necessity of that purchase 'squeezes out' other items
- Veblen goods – goods bought for ostentation

Price regulation

Some governments attempt to overcome market forces by **regulating prices**.

Maximum price

Used to combat inflation or make basic goods affordable

Minimum price

Used to secure incomes of favoured producers eg, farmers, oil

Price elasticity of demand (PED)

A measure of the change in **demand** for a good in response to a change in its **price**: when demand is **elastic** a small change in price produces a large change in demand. When the demand is inelastic, a large change in price produces only a small change in demand.

$$PED = \frac{\text{change in quantity demanded as \% of demand}}{\text{change in price as \% of price}} = \frac{\Delta Q}{Q} \times \frac{P}{\Delta P} = \frac{\Delta Q}{\Delta P} \times \frac{P}{Q}$$

P and Q may be values at a **point** or averages over an **arc**.

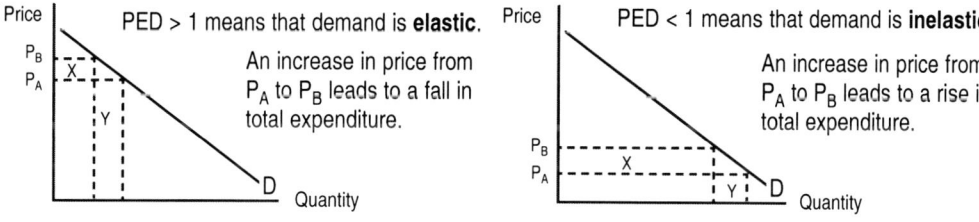

PED > 1 means that demand is **elastic**. An increase in price from P_A to P_B leads to a fall in total expenditure.

PED < 1 means that demand is **inelastic**. An increase in price from P_A to P_B leads to a rise in total expenditure.

| Full cost-plus pricing | Marginal cost-plus pricing | Mark-ups and margins | Demand and supply | Transfer pricing |

Factors affecting elasticity of supply

- Existence of inventory of all kinds of goods and their perishability
- Ease of adjusting labour inputs up or down
- Barriers to entry make supply inelastic
- Time scale

Factors affecting elasticity of demand

- Availability of substitutes
- Competitors pricing responses
- Necessities = inelastic, luxuries = elastic
- Percentage of income spent on a good – lower = more elastic
- Habit-forming goods = less elastic
- Time scale

Time factors

- Households may take a little time to respond to price but demand generally changes quicker than supply.
- During the **market period** only existing inventory and levels of output are available. Supply is **very inelastic.**
- Over the **short run**, quantities can be adjusted by working overtime or short time. Supply is **quite elastic.**
- Over the **long run** plant can be built or shut down. Supply is **very elastic.**

Income elasticity of demand

How demand for a good changes in response to changes in household income

% change in quantity demanded
—————————————————————
% change in household incomes

- \> 1 = income elastic ☐ luxury good
- < 0 = income inelastic ☐ inferior good
- 0 – 1 = income elastic ☐ necessity goods

Price elasticity of supply

How supply responds to a change in price

% change in quantity supplied
—————————————
% change in price

- 0 = perfectly inelastic supply ☐ fixed supply
- 1 = unit electricity ☐ proportionate variation of supply with price
- ☐ = perfect elasticity ☐ all is supplied at one price, none at any other price

Cross elasticity of demand

How demand for one good changes in response to a change in the price of another good (assuming no change in price of first good)

% change in quantity demanded of A
—————————————————
% change in price of B

- \> 0 = positive cross-elasticity ☐ substitutes
- < 0 = negative cross-elasticity ☐ complements
- 0 = unrelated goods

| Full cost-plus pricing | Marginal cost-plus pricing | Mark-ups and margins | Demand and supply | **Transfer pricing** |

Aims of transfer pricing

- Promote divisional autonomy
- Equitable divisional performance measurement
- Overall corporate profit maximisation

Transfer prices based on opportunity costs

Transfer price per unit = standard variable cost in the transferring division + opportunity cost to the organisation as a whole for supplying the unit internally.

Transfer prices based on market price

Where a perfect external market exists and unit variable costs and selling prices are constant, the ideal transfer price (ie, the opportunity cost of transfer) will be one of the following.

- External market price
- External market price less savings in selling costs

How to set transfer prices

1. Recognise the levels of output, external sales and internal transfers that are best for the company as a whole.

2. Arrive at a transfer price that ensures all divisions maximise their profits at this same level of output (ie, there should not be a more profitable opportunity for individual divisions).

Transfer prices based on cost

If there is **no external market**, the transfer price has to be based on cost.

1	**Standard or actual?**	The use of standard costs is fairer because if actual costs are used the transferring division has no incentive to control its costs – it can pass on its inefficiencies to the receiving division.
2	**Variable cost?**	The transferring division does not cover its fixed costs (although this problem can be overcome by central decisions or by some form of **dual pricing** or **two-part charging** system).
3	**Full cost?**	The transferring division makes no profit.
4	**Full cost plus?**	What margin will all parties perceive as fair?

**Goal congruent decisions will be made if the transfer price is set in the range where:
variable cost in the transferring division ≤ net marginal revenue in the receiving division**

8: Budgeting

Topic List

- Budget uses
- Steps in preparation
- Traditional budget problems
- Preparing forecasts
- Alternative approaches

*A budget is a **plan for the forthcoming period**.*

It shows the detail of authorised expenditure that may be incurred on each type of cost during the period.

The budget therefore acts as a plan and an authorisation for managers to incur costs in the period.

Budgets are also used to control spending or monitor variances.

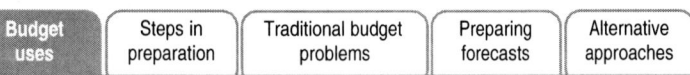

| Budget uses | Steps in preparation | Traditional budget problems | Preparing forecasts | Alternative approaches |

Uses of budgets

- Planning
- Communication
- Coordination
- Responsibility accounting
- Control
- Motivation

Budget = plan of what organisation intends to happen

Forecast = Prediction of what is likely to happen

Beyond budgeting

is an approach that suggests that budgets should be more adaptive and that this can be achieved by adopting 12 beyond budgeting principles:

Leadership principles	Management processes
- Purpose - Values - Transparency - Organisation - Autonomy - Customers	- Rhythm - Targets - Plans and forecasts - Resource allocation - Performance evaluation - Rewards

https://bbrt.org/wp-content/uploads/bb_principles.pdf

| Budget uses | **Steps in preparation** | Traditional budget problems | Preparing forecasts | Alternative approaches |

The order of budget preparation

The factor which limits the activities of an organisation

1 Identify the principal budget factor

2 Prepare a sales budget (units of product **and** sales value) and then a finished goods inventory budget (to determine the planned change in finished goods inventory levels)

3 Prepare a production budget (sales ± budgeted change in finished goods inventory levels, in units)

4 Prepare production resources budgets (materials usage, machine usage, labour)

5 Prepare a materials inventory budget (to determine the planned change in materials inventory levels)

6 Prepare a raw materials purchases budget in units and value (usage ± budgeted change in materials inventory)

7 Prepare overhead budgets

8 Prepare the **master budget (budgeted income statement, budgeted balance sheet, cash budget)**

| Budget uses | Steps in preparation | **Traditional budget problems** | Preparing forecasts | Alternative approaches |

Problems with traditional budgets

- Expensive
- Time consuming
- Quickly out-of-date
- Inflexible
- Based on inaccurate forecasts

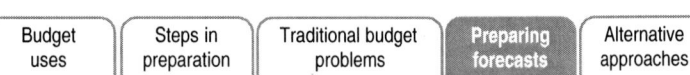

> A **forecast** is an estimate of what might happen in the future

Linear relationships

> A linear relationship can be expressed as $y = a + bx$.
>
> If there is a linear relationship between total cost and level of activity then
>
> y = total costs $\quad\quad$ a = fixed cost
>
> x = level of activity $\quad\quad$ b = unit variable cost

Cost forecasting with the high-low method

1. Select the periods with the highest and lowest activity levels.
2. Deduct the cost of the low activity level from the cost of the high activity level, and calculate the variable cost per unit (difference in variable costs ÷ difference in activity levels).
3. Calculate fixed cost (total cost at either output level − variable cost for output level chosen).
4. The linear equation $y = a + bx$ can be used to predict the cost for a given activity level.

Time series

is a series of observations recorded over time. The components are the trend, seasonal variations, cyclical variations and random variations.

Three main methods of finding a trend
- Line of best fit (trend line)
- Linear regression (least squares method)
- Moving averages

The moving averages method attempts to remove seasonal variations from actual data by the process of averaging, in order to identify the trend.

The additive model

$TS = T + SV$

where TS = actual time series
  T = trend series
  SV = seasonal component

The multiplicative model

$TS = T \times SV$

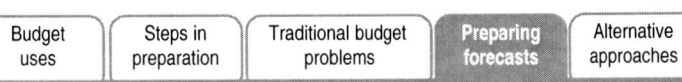

Moving averages – odd number of periods

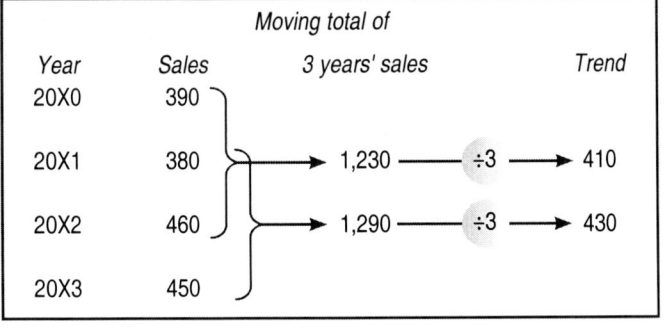

Machine learning

is the ability of a computational device to learn from large volumes of training data and improve upon a given task without having been explicitly programmed to do so.

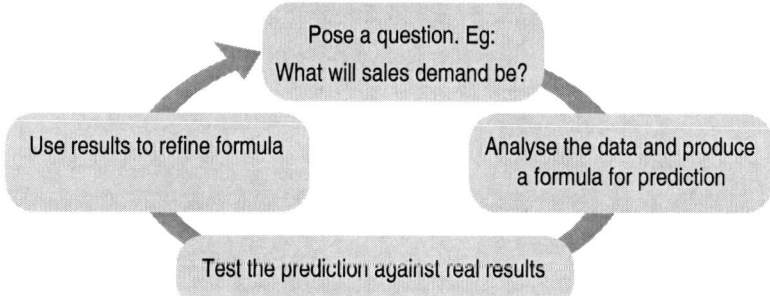

ML is used for forecasting.

Better forecasting leads to better management decision making.

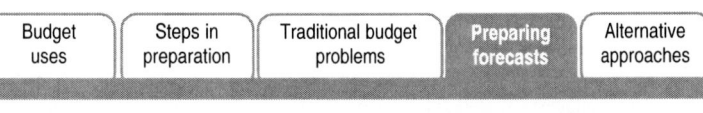

| Budget uses | Steps in preparation | Traditional budget problems | **Preparing forecasts** | Alternative approaches |

Other uses of AI

- Budget software population
- Expense tracking and insights
- Identifying seasonal variations
- Real-time alerts
- Scenario planning

Problems with AI

- Placing too much reliance on AI outputs
- High investment costs
- Data bias
- Ethical issues/copyright/data protection

| Budget uses | Steps in preparation | Traditional budget problems | Preparing forecasts | **Alternative approaches** |

Two budget-setting styles

- Imposed (from the top down)
- Participative (from the bottom up)

Participative approach

Advantages

- ☑ More realistic budgets
- ☑ Co-ordination, morale and motivation improved
- ☑ Increased management commitment to objectives

Disadvantages

- ☒ More time-consuming
- ☒ Budgetary slack may be introduced
- ☒ Does not suit some employees

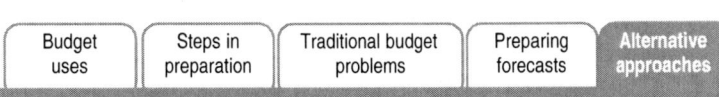

| Budget uses | Steps in preparation | Traditional budget problems | Preparing forecasts | **Alternative approaches** |

Imposed style

Advantages

- ☑ Include strategic plans
- ☑ Enhance co-ordination
- ☑ Reduce time taken to draw up budget
- ☑ Include senior management view

Disadvantages

- ☒ Low morale
- ☒ Acceptance of goals could be limited
- ☒ Stifle lower level initiative
- ☒ Team spirit may disappear

Incremental budgeting

involves adding a certain percentage to last year's budget to allow for growth/inflation.

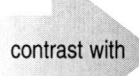
contrast with

ZBB

treats the preparation of the budget for each period as an independent planning exercise: the initial budget is zero and every item of expenditure has to be justified in its entirety to be included.

Advantages and disadvantages

Incremental
- ☑ Easy to prepare
- ☒ No incentive to try and reduce costs
- ☒ Budgetary slack and wasteful spending

ZBB
- ☑ (Hopefully) removes budgetary slack
- ☑ Identifies and removes inefficient and/or obsolete operations
- ☑ Forces employees to avoid wasteful expenditure
- ☒ Involves time and effort

| Budget uses | Steps in preparation | Traditional budget problems | Preparing forecasts | **Alternative approaches** |

Rolling budgets

Instead of preparing an annual budget for the full budget period, this process involves the preparation of budgets every one, two, three or four months. Each budget covers the next 12 months so that the current budget is extended by an extra period as the current period ends.

If a rolling budget is prepared every three months, the first three months of the period would be planned in great detail and the remaining nine months in less detail because of increased uncertainty about the longer-term future.

Why set rolling budgets?

- Effect of a suspected new competitor cannot be quantified when the budget is set
- Inflation is very high or is expected to rise/fall

Rolling budgets

Advantages

- ☑ They reduce uncertainty.
- ☑ An up-to-date budget is always available.
- ☑ Realistic budgets are better motivators.
- ☑ Planning/control is based on a recent plan.

Disadvantages

- ☒ They involve more time, effort and money.
- ☒ Frequent budgeting can have a detrimental effect on managers.

It might actually be simpler to update the annual budget once or twice during the year.

9: Working capital

Topic List

Working capital management

Cash operating cycle

Managing inventory

Managing payables and receivables

Treasury management

Cash budgets

The management of working capital components – inventory, payables, receivables, cash – is a very important part of managing a business's finances. Treasury management relates specifically to the management of the business's cash.

Working capital = Receivables + Inventory + Cash – Payables

Managing working capital

Hold cash to pay debts   ⟶   Liquidity vs profitability   ⟵   Invest cash to generate profit

Holding cash reduces   ⟶   Risk vs return   ⟵   Invest cash to generate profit
risk of insolvency

Remember that profit and cash flows are not the same. It is crucial for a business to maintain a sound liquidity position.

Working capital decisions

- Manipulate ratios to see effect of decision on risk/return
- Calculate revised cash operating cycles to see effect on liquidity
- Look at ratios/cycles used by similar companies

Solving liquidity problems

- Reduce inventory-holding period
- Reduce production period
- Reduce credit period for customers
- Improve cash collection
- Extend credit period from supplies (pay later)

| Working capital management | Cash operating cycle | Managing inventory | Managing payables and receivables | Treasury management | Cash budgets |

Working capital = current assets – current liabilities

Cash operating cycle

Cash operating cycle is the length of time between cash being spent at start of production and cash being received from customer.

=
Average time raw materials are in stock
Less: Period of credit taken from suppliers
Plus: Time taken to produce goods
Plus: Time taken by customers to pay for goods

- Retailers often receive cash, pay for supplies by credit
- Wholesalers mainly buy and sell on credit, need short-term borrowings
- Small companies may have trouble obtaining credit, but may have to offer generous credit terms

Useful ratios

Current ratio

$$= \frac{\text{Current assets}}{\text{Current liabilities}}$$

Quick (liquidity) ratio

$$= \frac{\text{Current assets excluding inventory}}{\text{Current liabilities}}$$

Average payables payment period

$$= \frac{\text{Average trades payables}}{\text{Annual purchases}} \times 365$$

Average receivables collection period

$$= \frac{\text{Average receivables}}{\text{Annual sales revenue}} \times 365$$

Averages should be used where available but year end figures should be used if not.

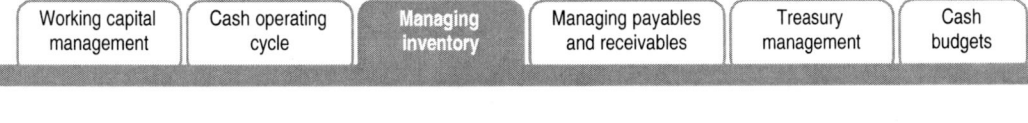

| Working capital management | Cash operating cycle | **Managing inventory** | Managing payables and receivables | Treasury management | Cash budgets |

Inventory

- Raw materials and components
- Spare parts/consumables
- Work-in-progress
- Finished goods
- Goods purchased for resale

Uses up cash but generates returns
Liquidity vs profitability

Reasons for holding inventory

- Buffer to meet demand
- Avoid risk of stockouts
- Avoid reliance on supplier lead times
- Ensure continuity of production
- Take advantage of quantity discounts and special promotions

- Buy at low price ahead of rises
- Order infrequently ☐ reduced ordering costs
- Seasonality of demand
- Suppliers insist on minimum order quantities

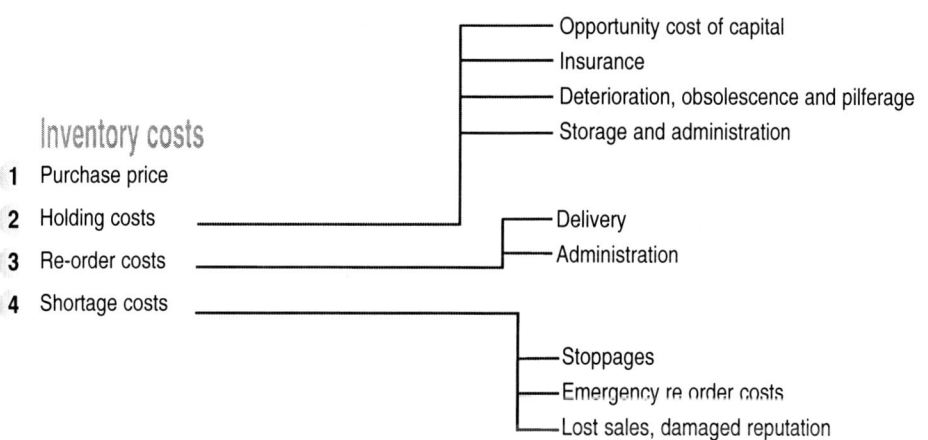

| Working capital management | Cash operating cycle | **Managing inventory** | Managing payables and receivables | Treasury management | Cash budgets |

Inventory control systems

- **Re-order level system** – the optimum quantity is ordered once inventory level reaches a certain level eg, two-bin system

- **Periodic review system** – levels are reviewed at certain points in time, and a variable amount is reordered at each point

- **ABC system** – A – high value/importance, closely monitored
  B – lower value/importance, less frequently monitored
  C – least important, not closely monitored

- **Just-in-time system** – deliveries flow straight through to production/resale, so minimum inventory is held. Requires flexibility, quality, close relations with suppliers and rationalised layouts

- **Perpetual inventory** – inventory movement in and out monitored on computer, with re-orders triggered automatically (expert system)

| Working capital management | Cash operating cycle | Managing inventory | **Managing payables and receivables** | Treasury management | Cash budgets |

Managing trade payables

Advantages of trade credit

- Convenient and informal
- Low cost
- Available to most businesses
- Settlement discount may be available
- Provides subsidy for new products
- Flexible in short-term

Costs of taking too long to pay

- Damaged credit status
- Raised prices to compensate suppliers
- Loss of discount for early payment

Ethics and sustainability

- Prompt payment relates to social and governance (ESG)
- Prompt payment is essential for a prosperous economy and long-term sustainability
- Late payment is unethical
- Payment processes should be clear

Improving payables management

- Weigh up value of credit period vs value of settlement discounts
- Negotiate better terms for large quantities
- Reconcile suppliers' statements carefully
- Pay only once delivery is complete
- Look for improved terms and consider switching

| Working capital management | Cash operating cycle | Managing inventory | **Managing payables and receivables** | Treasury management | Cash budgets |

Managing trade receivables

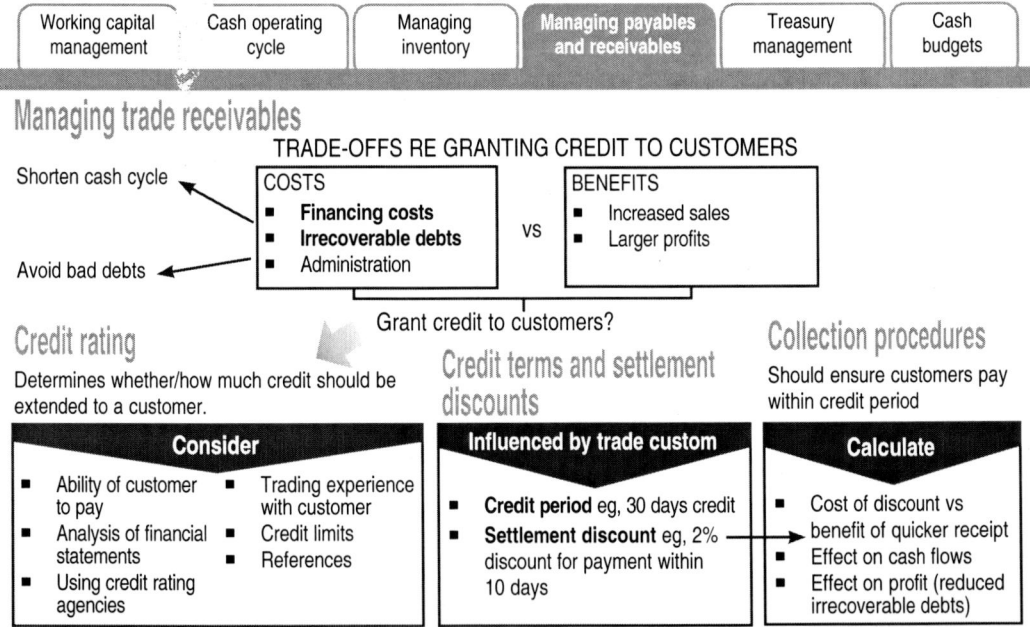

TRADE-OFFS RE GRANTING CREDIT TO CUSTOMERS

Shorten cash cycle →

Avoid bad debts →

COSTS
- **Financing costs**
- **Irrecoverable debts**
- Administration

vs

BENEFITS
- Increased sales
- Larger profits

Grant credit to customers?

Credit rating

Determines whether/how much credit should be extended to a customer.

Consider
- Ability of customer to pay
- Analysis of financial statements
- Using credit rating agencies
- Trading experience with customer
- Credit limits
- References

Credit terms and settlement discounts

Influenced by trade custom
- **Credit period** eg, 30 days credit
- **Settlement discount** eg, 2% discount for payment within 10 days

Collection procedures

Should ensure customers pay within credit period

Calculate
- Cost of discount vs benefit of quicker receipt
- Effect on cash flows
- Effect on profit (reduced irrecoverable debts)

Invoice discounting

Receivables factoring

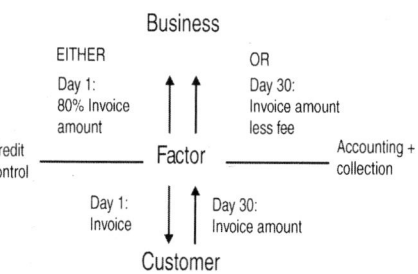

Managing receivables well

- Key accounts: 20:80 rule
- Reduce order ☐ sale time
- Invoice immediately/send credit notes promptly
- Reduce invoice ☐ collection time: monitor receivables ageing
- Personal contract
- Link sales commission to cash received, not invoices
- Set targets
- Take out credit insurance

| Working capital management | Cash operating cycle | Managing inventory | Managing payables and receivables | **Treasury management** | Cash budgets |

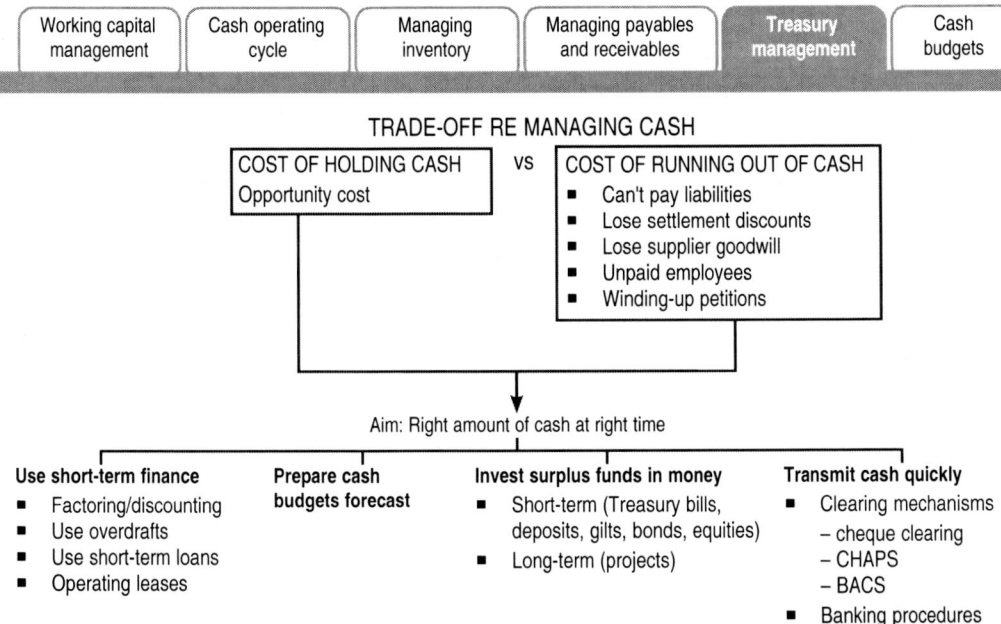

TRADE-OFF RE MANAGING CASH

COST OF HOLDING CASH	VS	COST OF RUNNING OUT OF CASH
Opportunity cost		■ Can't pay liabilities
		■ Lose settlement discounts
		■ Lose supplier goodwill
		■ Unpaid employees
		■ Winding-up petitions

Aim: Right amount of cash at right time

Use short-term finance
- Factoring/discounting
- Use overdrafts
- Use short-term loans
- Operating leases

Prepare cash budgets forecast

Invest surplus funds in money
- Short-term (Treasury bills, deposits, gilts, bonds, equities)
- Long-term (projects)

Transmit cash quickly
- Clearing mechanisms
  - cheque clearing
  - CHAPS
  - BACS
- Banking procedures

Capital markets

- **London Stock Exchange:**
  1. **Main market,** with firm regulation, for raising funds through new issues of shares (primary market), and trading existing shares (secondary market).
  2. **Alternative Investment Market:** for newer companies, less firmly regulated.
- **Gilt edged market** for UK government stock.
- **International capital markets** are operated between banks in larger countries to provide major finance for very large companies and institutions. Confusingly, their securities are known as eurobonds.
- Certain stocks not traded on recognised stock exchanges are traded in **over the counter** markets.

Money markets

Short-term investment and borrowing of funds is handled in the **money markets**. These are operated by the banks and other financial institutions and include markets for:

- Certificates of deposit
- Bills of exchange and commercial paper
- Treasury bills
- Building society bulk borrowing
- Local authority bills and other short-term borrowing

| Working capital management | Cash operating cycle | Managing inventory | Managing payables and receivables | Treasury management | **Cash budgets** |

A cash budget is a statement in which estimated future cash receipts and payments are tabulated in such a way as to show the forecast cash balance of a business at defined intervals.

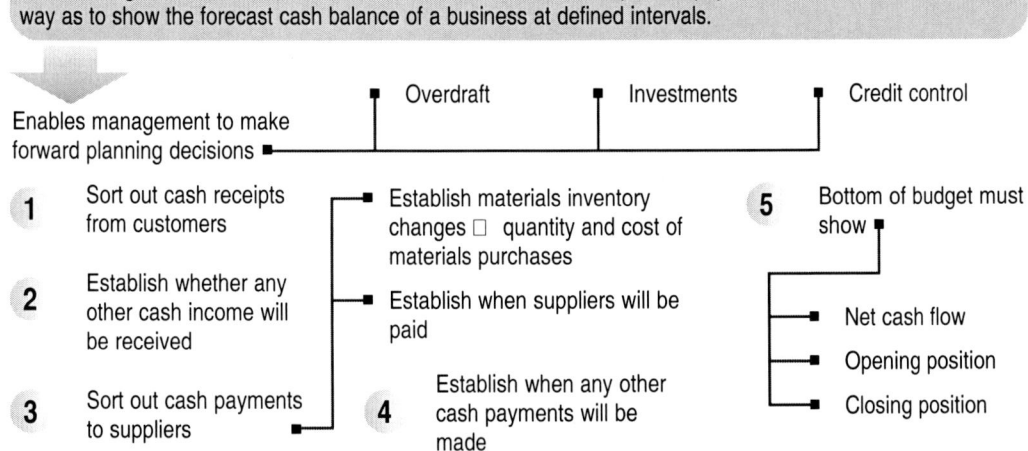

Enables management to make forward planning decisions ■

■ Overdraft   ■ Investments   ■ Credit control

1 Sort out cash receipts from customers

2 Establish whether any other cash income will be received

3 Sort out cash payments to suppliers

■ Establish materials inventory changes □ quantity and cost of materials purchases

■ Establish when suppliers will be paid

4 Establish when any other cash payments will be made

5 Bottom of budget must show ■

■ Net cash flow

■ Opening position

■ Closing position

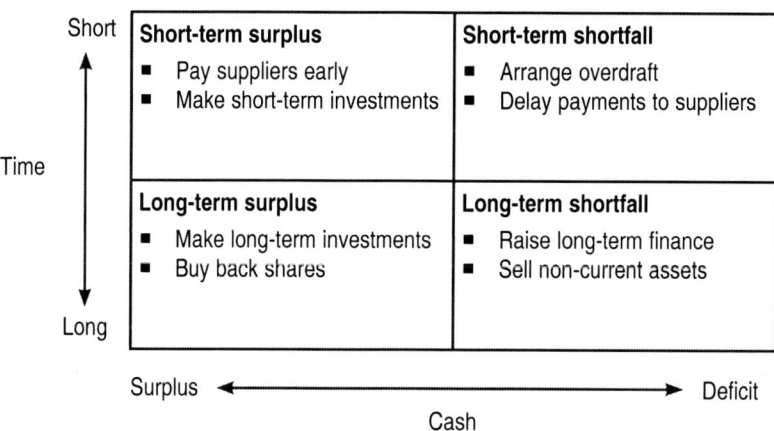

| Working capital management | Cash operating cycle | Managing inventory | Managing payables and receivables | Treasury management | **Cash budgets** |

PROFORMA CASH BUDGET

	Month 1 £	Month 2 £	Month 3 £
Cash receipts			
Receipts from customers	X	X	X
Loans etc	X	X	X
	$\overline{\overline{X}}$	$\overline{\overline{X}}$	$\overline{\overline{X}}$
Cash payments			
Payments to suppliers	X	X	X
Wages etc	X	X	X
	$\overline{\overline{X}}$	$\overline{\overline{X}}$	$\overline{\overline{X}}$
Net cash flow (receipts – payments)	X	X	X
Opening balance	X	X	X
Closing balance	$\overline{\overline{X}}$	$\overline{\overline{X}}$	$\overline{\overline{X}}$

10: Standard costing and variance analysis

Topic List

Budgetary control

Standard costs and costing

Cost variances

Sales variances and operating statements

Interpreting variances and actual costs

*In a standard costing system, standard costs are devised for each cost unit for **price** and **quantity** of resources used.*

This allows comparisons to be made with actual results and variances are calculated.

These variances can be interpreted and action taken as needed.

| Budgetary control | Standard costs and costing | Cost variances | Sales variances and operating statements | Interpreting variances and actual costs |

Fixed budgets

These are budgets which are set for a single activity level. Master budgets are fixed budgets.

VS

Flexible budgets

These are budgets which, by recognising different cost behaviours patterns, change as activity levels change.

Using flexible budgets for control

1 Produce a flexible budget based on the **actual** activity level

2 Compare the flexible budget with the fixed budget, and with actual results

3 Identify variances

Volume variance = difference between fixed budget and flexible budget

Expenditure variance = difference between flexible budget and actual results

To **prepare a flexible budget**:

1 Decide whether costs are fixed, variable or semi-variable, and split semi-variable costs using the high/low method

2 Calculate the budget cost allowance for each item = budgeted fixed cost* + (number of units × variable cost per unit)**

* nil for variable cost   ** nil for fixed cost

| Budgetary control | **Standard costs and costing** | Cost variances | Sales variances and operating statements | Interpreting variances and actual costs |

Standard costing

is a control technique that reports variances by comparing actual costs to pre-set standards so facilitating action through management by exception.

Uses

- To value inventories and cost production
- To act as a control device via variance analysis

Standard costs

The total standard cost of a product is built up from standards for each cost element. These must be monitored to ensure that they are reasonable and reliable.

Advantages

- ☑ Aid accurate budgeting
- ☑ Yard stick for measuring actual costs
- ☑ Promote **cost consciousness**
- ☑ Simplify bookkeeping
- ☑ Provide incentives for employees

Budgetary control	Standard costs and costing	Cost variances	Sales variances and operating statements	Interpreting variances and actual costs

STANDARD COST CARD
PRODUCT LW

	£
Direct material (standard quantity □ standard price)	X
Direct labour (standard time □ standard rate)	X
Standard direct cost	X
Variable production overhead (standard time □ standard rate)	X
Standard variable cost of production	X
Fixed production overhead (standard time □ standard rate)	X
Standard full production cost	X
Administration and marketing overhead	X
Standard cost of sale	X
Standard profit	X
Standard selling price	X

| Budgetary control | Standard costs and costing | **Cost variances** | Sales variances and operating statements | Interpreting variances and actual costs |

Direct material total variance

	£
1,000 units should have cost	100,000
but did cost	98,600
Direct material total variance	1,400 (F)

Example

Product LW has a standard direct material cost as follows:

10 kg of material M at £10 per kg = £100 per unit of M

During a period, 1,000 units of LW were manufactured, using 11,700 kg of material M, which cost £98,600.

Direct material price

	£
11,700 kg of M should have cost	117,000
but did cost	98,600
Material M price variance	18,400 (F)

Direct material usage

1,000 units should have used (□ 10 kg)	10,000 kg
but did use	11,700 kg
Usage variance in kgs	1,700 kg (A)
□ standard cost per kilogram	□ £10
Material M usage variance	£17,000 (A)

Direct material cost variance = material price variance + material usage variance

Page 117

10: Standard cost

| Budgetary control | Standard costs and costing | **Cost variances** | Sales variances and operating statements | Interpreting variances and actual costs |

Direct labour total variance

	£
1,500 units of product LW	
should have cost ($\times$ £10)	15,000
but did cost	17,500
Direct labour total variance	2,500 (A)

Direct labour rate variance

	£
3,080 hours of grade A labour	
should have cost ($\times$ £5)	15,400
but did cost	17,500
Direct labour rate variance	2,100 (A)

Example

The standard direct labour cost of product LW is as follows.

2 hours of grade A labour at £5 per hour = £10 per unit of product LW

During a period, 1,500 units of product LW were made, and the direct labour cost of grade A labour was £17,500 for 3,080 hours of work.

Direct labour efficiency variance

1,500 units of product LW	
should take ($\times$ 2 hours)	3,000 hrs
but did take (3,080)	3,080 hrs
Direct labour efficiency variance in hrs	80 hrs (A)
$\times$ standard rate per hour	$\times$ £5
Direct labour efficiency variance in £	400 (A)

Direct labour total variance = labour rate variance + labour efficiency variance

Variable production overhead variances

Variable overhead total variance

	£
400 units	
should cost (□ £3)	1,200
but did cost	1,360
Total variance	160 (A)

Expenditure variance

	£
820 hours of var. prod. o'head	
should cost (□ £1.50)	1,230
but did cost	1,360
Variable production overhead expenditure variance	130 (A)

> **Example**
>
> The variable production overhead cost of product LW is as follows:
>
> 2 hours @ £1.50 = £3 per unit
>
> During a period, 400 units of product LW were made. The labour force worked 820 hours. The variable overhead cost was £1,360.

Efficiency variance

400 units of product LW should take (□ 2 hrs)	800 hrs
but did take (active)	820 hrs
Variable prod. o'head efficiency variance in hours	20 hrs (A)
□ standard rate per hour	□ £1.50
Variable production overhead efficiency variance in £	£30 (A)

| Budgetary control | Standard costs and costing | Cost variances | Sales variances and operating statements | Interpreting variances and actual costs |

Fixed overhead expenditure variance

is simply the difference between the budgeting and actual fixed overhead expenditure in the period.

= Budgeting fixed overhead cost – Actual fixed overhead cost

| Budgetary control | Standard costs and costing | Cost variances | **Sales variances and operating statements** | Interpreting variances and actual costs |

Selling price variance

is a measure of the effect on expected revenue of a different selling price to standard selling price.

Example

The standard selling price of product H is £15. Actual sales in 2001 were 2,000 units at £15.30 per unit. Budgeted sales were 2,200 units and standard variable cost per unit of H is £12.30.

Sales volume variance

is the difference between actual units sold and the budgeted quantity, valued at the standard contribution per unit.

Selling price variance   £
Sales revenue from 2,000 units
  should have been (× £15)   30,000
  but was (× £15.30)   30,600
Selling price variance   600 (F)

Favourable variance because the price was higher than expected

Sales volume variance
Budgeted sales volume   2,200
Actual sales volume   2,000
                                                    200 (A)
× standard contribution per unit
  (£15 – £12.30)   × £2.70
Sales volume variance   540 (A)

Adverse variance because actual sales volume was less than budgeted

10: Standard costing and variance analysis

Budgetary control	Standard costs and costing	Cost variances	Sales variances and operating statements	Interpreting variances and actual costs

An operating statement is a regular report for management of actual cost and revenues, as appropriate. It will usually compare actual with budget to show variances.

OPERATING STATEMENT

	£
Budgeted contribution	X
Sales volume variance	X
Sales price variance	X
Actual sales less standard variable cost of sales	X

VARIABLE COST VARIANCES	Favourable	Adverse	
	£	£	£
Material price	X		
Material usage etc		X	
Total variable cost variances	X	X	X
ACTUAL CONTRIBUTION			X

		£	
Budgeted fixed overhead		X	
Fixed overhead expenditure variance		X	
Actual fixed overhead			X
Actual profit			X

> Operating statements sometimes reconcile budgeted profit to actual profit.

OPERATING STATEMENT

	Favourable £	Adverse £	£
Budgeted profit			X
Sales volume variance		X	
Sales price variance	X		
COST VARIANCES			
Materials price	X		
Materials usage		X	
Labour rate		X	
Labour efficiency		X	
Variable overhead rate		X	
Variable overhead efficiency		X	
Fixed overhead expenditure		X	
TOTAL VARIANCES	X	X	X
Actual profit			X

| Budgetary control | Standard costs and costing | Cost variances | Sales variances and operating statements | **Interpreting variances and actual costs** |

Material price

Favourable	Adverse
Unforeseen discounts	Price increase
Material std changed	Careless purchasing

Variable and fixed overhead

Favourable	Adverse
Cost savings	Excessive use

Sales price

Favourable	Adverse
Original selling price too low	Original selling price too high

Material usage

Favourable	Adverse
Higher quality material	Defective material
Effective use of material	Excessive waste

Labour rate

Favourable	Adverse
Lower rate paid	Wage rate increase

Labour efficiency

Favourable	Adverse
Motivated staff	Lack of training

Sales volume

Favourable	Adverse
Efficient sales force	Demotivated sales force

Interdependence

The cause of one variance (adverse) might be wholly or partly explained by the cause of another favourable variance.

- Material price and usage variances
- Material price and labour efficiency variances
- Labour rate and efficiency variances
- Sales price and sales volume
- Cost and sales variance

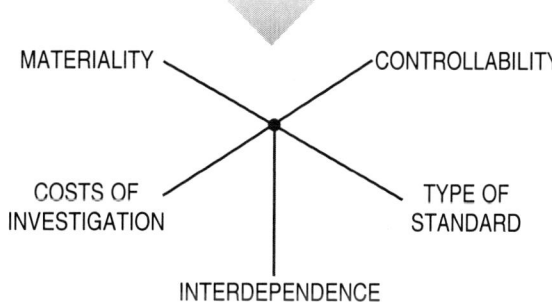

Significant variances should be investigated. Factors to take into account:

- MATERIALITY
- CONTROLLABILITY
- TYPE OF STANDARD
- INTERDEPENDENCE
- COSTS OF INVESTIGATION

Data bias may occur in variance analysis and professional scepticism should be applied – eg by presenting comparative variance information to interpret variances fairly.

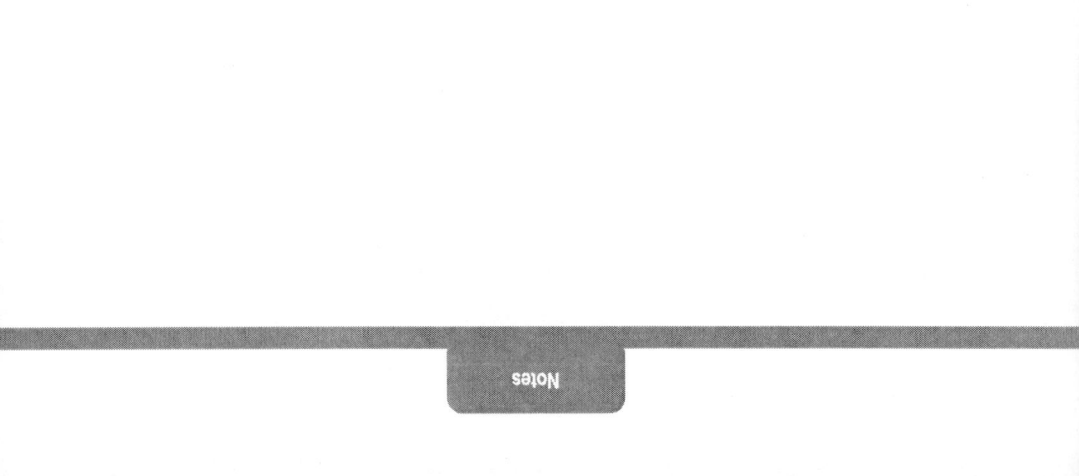

11: Breakeven analysis and limiting factor analysis

Topic List

Breakeven analysis and contribution

Breakeven charts

Limiting factor analysis

Managers need to be aware of how costs change when decisions are made. They can then work out measures such as the activity required to break even.

Understanding the contribution earned by products and services will also help managers to allocate scarce resources to maximise contribution.

| Breakeven analysis and contribution | Breakeven charts | Limiting factor analysis |

Contribution per unit

is unit selling price – unit variable costs.

Contribution ratio

is a measure of how much contribution is earned from each £1 of sales revenue.

Breakeven point

is activity level at which there is neither profit nor loss.

$$\frac{\text{Total fixed costs}}{\text{Contribution per unit}} \quad \Longleftarrow \quad \boxed{\text{Breakeven point}} \quad \Longrightarrow \quad \frac{\text{Contribution required to break even}}{\text{Contribution ratio}}$$

Sales revenue at breakeven point

The margin of safety is the difference in units between the budgeted sales volume and the breakeven sales volume and it is sometimes expressed as a percentage of the budgeted sales volume.

The sales volume to achieve a target profit = $\dfrac{\text{Fixed costs + target profit}}{\text{Contribution per unit}}$

Example

Selling price = £15 per unit
Variable cost = £12 per unit
Fixed costs = £5,400 per annum
Budgeted sales pa = 3,000 units

- Breakeven point (units) = $\dfrac{£5,400}{£15 - £12}$ = 1,800 units

- Contribution ratio = 3/15 × 100% = 20% = 0.2

- Breakeven point (revenue) = $\dfrac{5,400}{0.2}$ = £27,000

- Sales volume to achieve profit of £3,300 = $\dfrac{£(5,400 + 3,300)}{£3}$ = 2,900 units

- Margin of safety (as a %) = $\dfrac{3,000 - 1,800}{3,000}$ × 100% = 40%

| Breakeven analysis and contribution | **Breakeven charts** | Limiting factor analysis |

Breakeven chart

Shows the approximate level of profit or loss at different sales volume levels within a limited range.

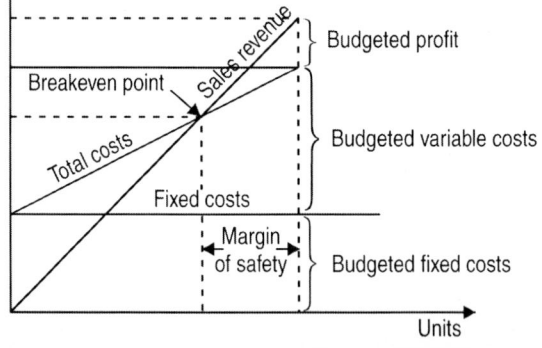

- Profit/loss is the difference between the sales revenue line and the total costs line.

- The breakeven point is where the total costs line and the sales revenue line meet.

Contribution breakeven chart

> Shows the variable costs line instead of the fixed costs line.

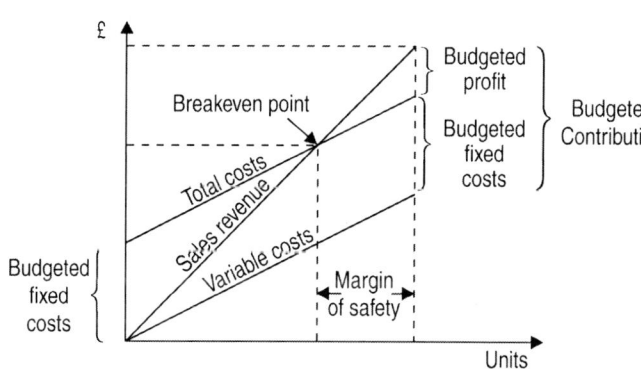

- This type of chart shows clearly the contribution for different levels of production

- At the breakeven point, contribution = fixed costs

- Contribution = Sales revenue line – variable costs line

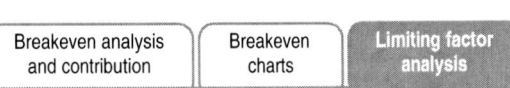

| Breakeven analysis and contribution | Breakeven charts | Limiting factor analysis |

Limiting factor situations

Scenario	How to maximise contribution/profit	Detail
Sales demand restricts greater production/output	Make exactly the amount required for sales (and no more) provided that each product sold earns a positive contribution	
One scarce resource (such as material or labour)	Earn the biggest possible contribution per unit of scarce resource	Assume fixed costs remain unchanged whatever the production mix, the only relevant costs being variable costs
One limiting factor and restrictions on sales demand or two potentially limiting factors	Rank products in order of contribution-earning ability per unit of limiting factor but produce the top-ranked products up to the sales demand limit	Although there may appear to be more than one scarce resource, it may be that there is no limiting factor except sales demand or that there is only one scarce resource that prevents full potential sales demand being achieved

Profit will be maximised when contribution is maximised.

The profit-maximising product mix might not be possible because the mix is also restricted by a factor other than a scarce resource.

In such circumstances the organisation might have to produce more of a particular product or products than the level established by ranking according to contribution per unit of limiting factor.

Factors that restrict freedom of action

- A contract to supply a certain number of products
- Provision of a complete product range and/or maintenance of customer goodwill
- Maintenance of a certain market share

Basic approach

1. Confirm that the limiting factor is not sales demand
2. Rank the products in the normal way
3. Take account of the minimum production requirements within the optimum production plan
4. Allocate the remaining resources according to the ranking

| | | | Breakeven analysis and contribution | | Breakeven charts | | **Limiting factor analysis** |

Make or buy decisions and scarce resources

Suppose a company must subcontract work to make up a shortfall in its own production capacity.

Its total costs are minimised if those units bought have the lowest extra variable cost of buying per unit of scarce resource saved.

Example

A company, which makes three products, has limited labour time available:

	A	B	C
	£	£	£
Variable cost of making	10	16	14
Variable cost of buying	19	20	19
Extra variable cost of buying	9	4	5
Labour hours saved by buying (per unit)	3	2	2
Extra variable cost of buying per hour saved	£3	£2	£2.50
Priority for making in-house	1st	3rd	2nd

12: Investment appraisal techniques

Topic List

Investment appraisal decisions

Payback

Accounting rate of return

Net present value (NPV)

Internal rate of return (IRR)

Environmental costs

Capital expenditure differs from revenue expenditure. Thus:

- *It involves a larger outlay of cash*
- *Benefits accrue over a long period of time*

There are several techniques that are available to make capital spending decisions. These range in their usefulness. Make sure you know where each technique is most suitable to use.

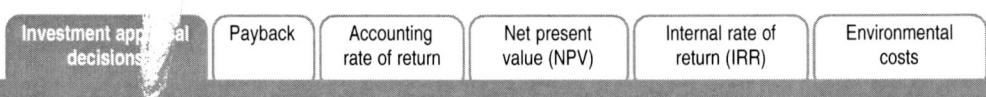

Investment decision-making process

1 Origination of proposals

Set up a mechanism which scans the environment for potential opportunities and provides an early warning of future problems.

2 Project screening

Carry out a qualitative evaluation:

- Purpose
- 'Fit' with long-term objectives
- Alternatives

3 Analysis and acceptance

- Submit standard format financial information as a formal investment proposal
- Consider qualitative and quantitative issues
- Carry out **financial analysis**

4 Monitoring and review

- Control over excess spending
- Control over delays
- Control over anticipated benefits

| Investment appraisal decisions | **Payback** | Accounting rate of return | Net present value (NPV) | Internal rate of return (IRR) | Environmental costs |

Payback

The time it takes the cash inflows (☐ **profits before depreciation**) from an investment to equal the cash outflows, usually expressed in years.

It is often used as a first screening method, the project being evaluated with a more sophisticated technique if it gets through the payback test.

Decision rules

- When deciding between two or more competing projects, the usual decision is to accept the one with the shortest payback.
- Reject a project if its payback is greater than a target payback.

| Investment appraisal decisions | **Payback** | Accounting rate of return | Net present value (NPV) | Internal rate of return (IRR) | Environmental costs |

Disadvantages

- ☒ It ignores the timing of cash flows within the payback period, the cash flows after the end of the payback period and hence the total project return.
- ☒ It ignores the time value of money.
- ☒ It makes no distinction between different projects with the same payback period.
- ☒ The choice of cut-off payback period is arbitrary.
- ☒ The method may lead to excessive investment in short-term projects.
- ☒ It takes account of the risk associated with the timing of cash flows but not the variability of those cash flows.

Advantages

- ☑ Long payback means capital is tied up.
- ☑ A focus on early payback can enhance liquidity.
- ☑ Investment risk is increased if payback is longer.
- ☑ Shorter-term forecasts are likely to be more reliable.
- ☑ The calculation is quick and simple.
- ☑ Payback is an easily understood concept.

| Investment appraisal decisions | Payback | **Accounting rate of return** | Net present value (NPV) | Internal rate of return (IRR) | Environmental costs |

Accounting rate of return (ARR)

There are several definitions of ARR (the method selected should be used consistently) but the two recommended definitions are:

$$ARR = \frac{\text{Average annual accounting profit}}{\text{Average investment}} \times 100\%$$

$$ARR = \frac{\text{Average annual accounting profit}}{\text{Initial investment}} \times 100\%$$

- **Annual profits are after depreciation**
- Average investment = ½ (initial cost + residual value)

If you are not provided with a figure for profit, assume that net cash inflow minus depreciation equals profit.

Decision rules

- **One project**
  - If the ARR is greater than the target rate of return, accept the project.
  - If the ARR is less than the target rate of return, reject the project.

- **When comparing two or more mutually exclusive projects, the project with the highest ARR should be chosen (provided the ARR is greater than the target ARR).**

| Investment appraisal decisions | Payback | **Accounting rate of return** | Net present value (NPV) | Internal rate of return (IRR) | Environmental costs |

Advantages

- ☑ Quick and simple
- ☑ Looks at the entire project life
- ☑ Easily calculated from financial statements
- ☑ An appraisal method that employs profit may be more easily understood

Disadvantages

- ☒ Takes no account of the timing of cash flows
- ☒ Based on accounting profits which are subject to a number of different accounting treatments
- ☒ Takes no account of the size of the investment or the length of the project
- ☒ Ignores the time value of money

Example

Equipment J has a capital cost of £100,000 and a disposal value of £20,000 at the end of its five-year life. Profits before depreciation over the five years total £150,000.

☐ Total profit after depreciation = £(150,000 – 80,000) = £70,000

Average annual profit after depreciation = £14,000

(Capital cost + disposal cost) / 2 = £60,000

ARR = (14/60) ☐ 100% = 20%

| Investment appraisal decisions | Payback | Accounting rate of return | **Net present value (NPV)** | Internal rate of return (IRR) | Environmental costs |

Present value

The cash equivalent now (X) of a sum of money (V) receivable or payable at the end of n time periods.

Discounting provides the formula $X = V/(1+r)^n$, where r is the rate of return.

Compounding provides the formula $V = X(1+r)^n$ which is the **terminal value** of an investment.

Net present value

The value obtained by discounting all cash inflows and outflows of a capital investment project by a chosen target rate of return.

Organisations may use different discount rates over the life of a project to reflect interest and inflation.

Decision rules

- **One project**
  - If NPV > 0 ▸ accept project
  - If NPV < 0 ▸ reject project

- **When comparing two or more mutually exclusive projects, the project with the highest positive NPV should be selected.**

Investment appraisal decisions	Payback	Accounting rate of return	**Net present value (NPV)**	Internal rate of return (IRR)	Environmental costs

Time value of money

Why is £1 now worth more than £1 in the future?

- Uncertainty
- Inflation
- More weight is attached to current pleasures than to those occurring in the future

Discount factors

Present value tables cover integer costs of capital from 1% to 20% for 1 to 20 years. If you require a discount factor for a non-integer interest rate (say 12.5%) or a period of time greater than 20 years, use $1/(1+r)^n$, where r = cost of capital and n = number of years

Timing of cash flows

- A cash outlay to be incurred at the beginning of an investment project ('**now**') occurs at time 0 and will have a present value = outlay (since PV of £1 now = £1)
- A cash flow occurring **during the course of a time period** is assumed to occur at the end of the time period
- A cash flow occurring **at the beginning of a time period** is assumed to occur at the end of the previous time period

Perpetuities

An annual cash flow in perpetuity. (An annuity that lasts forever.)

The PV of £1 pa in perpetuity at r% = £1/r (where r is a decimal).

Net terminal value (NTV)

The cash surplus remaining at the end of a project after taking account of interest and capital repayments.

The NTV discounted at the cost of capital = NPV

Other aspects of discounting

1 Delayed annuities **2** Annuities in advance

Annuities

A constant annual cash flow from year to year.

Use discount factors from **cumulative present value tables.**

Discounted payback

combines **payback** with **DCF** to calculate a **discounted payback period (DPP).**

The DPP is the time it will take before a project's cumulative NPV turns from being negative to being positive.

| Investment appraisal decisions | Payback | Accounting rate of return | Net present value (NPV) | Internal rate of return (IRR) | Environmental costs |

IRR

The rate of interest at which the NPV of an investment is zero.

Decision rule

If the IRR is greater than the target rate of return, the project is worth undertaking.

IRR of a perpetuity

- IRR = perpetuity ÷ initial investment

Graphical approach

Suppose a project has the following NPVs at the following discount rates.

Discount rate	NPV
%	£
5	5,300
10	2,900
15	(1,700)
20	(3,200)

These can be easily plotted on a graph.

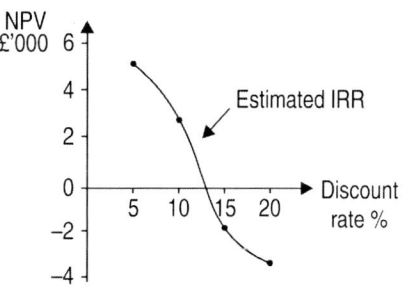

Recalculate the NPV using the estimated IRR (from the graph) of 13% and if the resulting NPV is not equal to, or very near, zero, additional NPVs at different discount rates should be calculated, the graph redrawn and a more accurate IRR determined.

| Investment appraisal decisions | Payback | Accounting rate of return | Net present value (NPV) | Internal rate of return (IRR) | Environmental costs |

Interpolation method

1 Calculate the NPV using a rough indicator of the IRR ($^2/_3$ (or $^3/_4$) $\Box$ ARR).

Remember, you will need to account for depreciation and any residual value when determining the ARR.

2 If the resulting NPV > 0, recalculate the NPV using a higher rate.

3 If the resulting NPV < 0, recalculate the NPV using a lower rate.

The closer these NPVs are to zero, the closer the estimate to the true IRR.

4 $$IRR = a + \frac{NPVa}{NPVa - NPVb} (b - a)$$

where a is the first discount rate giving NPVa
b is the second discount rate giving NPVb

NPV vs IRR

	Which is better?	
	NPV	**IRR**
- When cash flow patterns are conventional both methods give the same accept or reject decision	☑	☑
- The IRR method is more easily understood		☑
- IRR and ROCE/ROI can be confused	☑	
- IRR ignores the relative sizes of investments	☑	
- When cash flow patterns are non-conventional there may be several IRRs of which decision makers must be aware to avoid making the wrong decision	☑	
- The NPV method is superior for ranking mutually exclusive projects in order of attractiveness	☑	
- When discount rates are expected to differ over the life of the project, such variations can be incorporated easily into NPV calculations but not into IRR calculations	☑	

Despite the advantages of the NPV method over the IRR method, the IRR method is widely used in practice.

| Investment appraisal decisions | Payback | Accounting rate of return | Net present value (NPV) | Internal rate of return (IRR) | Environmental costs |

Environmental prevention costs

These are the costs required to eliminate environmental impacts before they occur – eg, forming environmental policies.

Environmental appraisal costs

These are the costs involved with establishing whether activities are complying with environmental standards and policies – eg, monitoring, testing and inspection costs.

Environmental internal failure costs

These are the costs of activities that must be undertaken when contaminants and waste have been created by a business but not released into the environment – eg, maintaining pollution equipment.

Environmental external failure costs

These are the costs that arise when a business releases harmful waste into the environment – eg, cleaning up oil spills.

Note that organisations with good ESG policies are seen as having lower risk by banks and investors.

13: The external environment of business

Topic List

- The macroeconomic environment
- Market structure
- Free markets and market failure
- Regulation of business
- Regulation of competition
- Regulation of business people

The economic environment of a business is determined by the forces of supply and demand, and by government regulation. Governments intervene in markets to address market failures, and to protect the public interest.

| The macroeconomic environment | Market structure | Free markets and market failure | Regulation of business | Regulation of competition | Regulation of business people |

Economics

The production and consumption of goods and services: what to produce, how to produce it and who to produce it for

The production of goods and services requires the utilisation of economic **resources** or **factors of production**. These resources are **scarce** and therefore choices must be made to how they are to be employed.

- **LAND** includes all **natural resources**. Land itself is limited in quantity but can be improved in quality.
- **LABOUR** is people employed to produce goods and services. It varies in quality.
- **CAPITAL** consists of physical goods that aid production. Money can be transformed into capital.
- **ENTERPRISE** is needed both to organise production and to take the risk of possible financial loss.

A market

Potential buyers and potential sellers come together for the purpose of exchange

Market structure

The number of buyers and sellers in a market and their relative bargaining power

The firm

Sellers are **firms**; buyers of consumer goods and services are **households**

Microeconomic environment

How the market mechanism of the interaction of supply and demand for an item affects a particular firm

Macroeconomic environment

The world in which all firms operate, incorporating global and national influences

The macroeconomic environment	Market structure	Free markets and market failure	Regulation of business	Regulation of competition	Regulation of business people

Role of government in the national economy

- **Producer**, of certain goods and services
- **Purchaser**, of final goods and services
- **Investment**, in roads, schools, hospitals etc
- **Transfer payments**, between one section of the economy and another

Factors affecting consumption in an economy

- Changes in disposable income
- Changes in distribution of wealth
- Government policy
- Development of major new products
- Interest rates
- Price expectations

The business cycle

The **four main phases** of the **business cycle** are:

- **Recession (A)**
- **Depression (B)**
- **Recovery (C)**
- **Boom (D)**

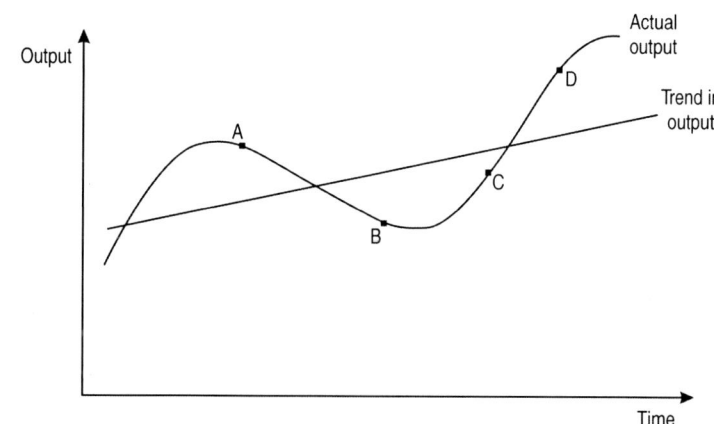

| The macroeconomic environment | Market structure | Free markets and market failure | Regulation of business | Regulation of competition | Regulation of business people |

Inflation

An increase in price levels generally, and a decline in the purchasing power of money

Why is inflation a problem?

- Redistribution of income and wealth
- Balance of payments effects
- Price signalling and 'noise'
- Wage bargaining
- Consumer behaviour

Monetary policy

Government policies on the money supply, monetary system, interest rates, exchange rates and the availability of credit

Quantitative easing

A form of expansionary monetary policy which involves the central bank (Bank of England in the UK) buying existing government bonds (gilts) and corporate bonds as a way of adding liquidity to the financial system.

Fiscal policy

Government policies on taxation, public borrowing and public spending

Supply-side policies

- Involve the private sector
- Reduce taxes
- Cut power of unions
- Improve education and training
- Increase competition
- Deregulate markets

| The macroeconomic environment | **Market structure** | Free markets and market failure | Regulation of business | Regulation of competition | Regulation of business people |

Types of market structure

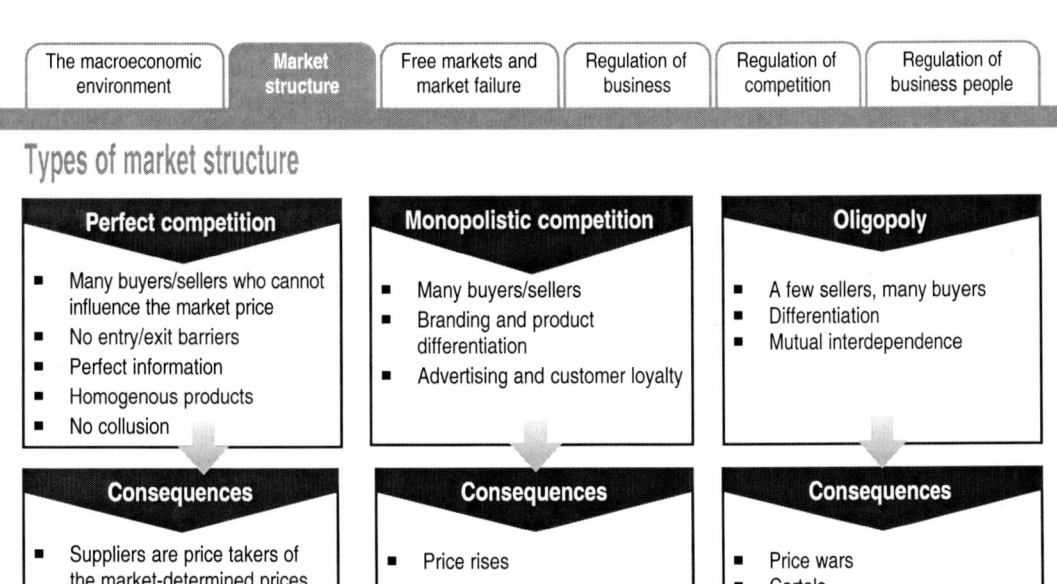

Perfect competition

- Many buyers/sellers who cannot influence the market price
- No entry/exit barriers
- Perfect information
- Homogenous products
- No collusion

Consequences

- Suppliers are price takers of the market-determined prices
- Normal profits
- Single selling price

Monopolistic competition

- Many buyers/sellers
- Branding and product differentiation
- Advertising and customer loyalty

Consequences

- Price rises

Oligopoly

- A few sellers, many buyers
- Differentiation
- Mutual interdependence

Consequences

- Price wars
- Cartels

Monopoly

- One supplier, many buyers
- Barriers to entry

Types of monopoly

- Pure monopoly – only one supplier
- Actual monopoly – one dominant supplier
- Government franchise monopoly
- Natural monopoly – economies of scale

Duopoly

- Two dominant sellers control prices

Consequences

- Monopoly **either** sets the market price **or** the quantity supplied
- Supernormal profits

Consequences

- High prices
- Cartels

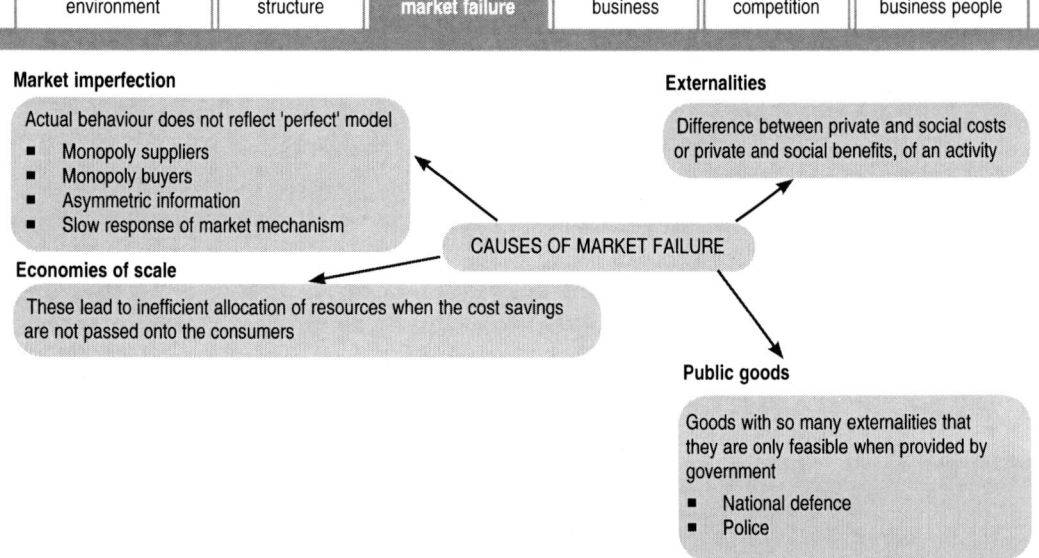

| The macroeconomic environment | Market structure | Free markets and market failure | Regulation of business | Regulation of competition | Regulation of business people |

Market imperfection

Actual behaviour does not reflect 'perfect' model

- Monopoly suppliers
- Monopoly buyers
- Asymmetric information
- Slow response of market mechanism

Economies of scale

These lead to inefficient allocation of resources when the cost savings are not passed onto the consumers

CAUSES OF MARKET FAILURE

Externalities

Difference between private and social costs or private and social benefits, of an activity

Public goods

Goods with so many externalities that they are only feasible when provided by government

- National defence
- Police

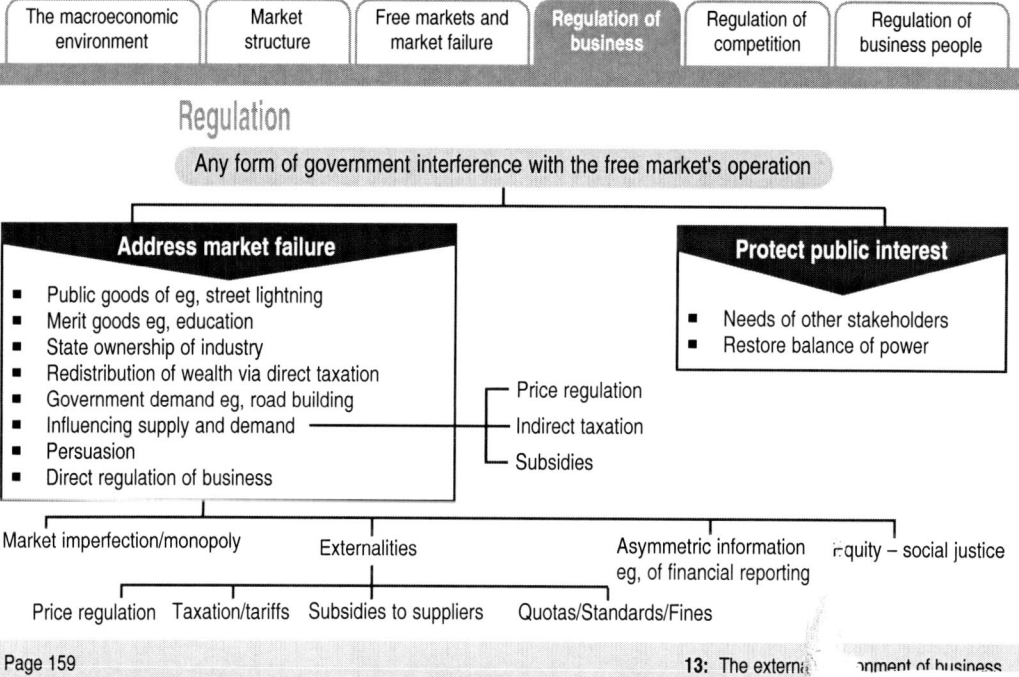

| The macroeconomic environment | Market structure | Free markets and market failure | **Regulation of business** | Regulation of competition | Regulation of business people |

Potential responses of business

- **Entrenchment** – non-response
- **Mere compliance** – cost of compliance passed on to customers
- **Full compliance** – change in behaviour
- **Innovation** – the Porter hypothesis. Environmental regulation triggers discovery/introduction of cleaner technologies and environmental improvements

Efficient regulation: total benefits > total costs

Outcomes of business regulation

- Address market failure
- Change social standing of certain groups
- Implement desires of majority
- Increase diversity
- Deal with irreversibility

Regulatory bodies

- FRC
- FCA
- PRA
- Competition and Markets Authority (CMA)

| The macroeconomic environment | Market structure | Free markets and market failure | Regulation of business | **Regulation of competition** | Regulation of business people |

Aim: To prevent the concentration of power in one or two suppliers. Maximum fine for breaching prohibitions 10% worldwide revenue.

1 Prohibition of anti-competitive agreements

Prohibited regardless of size of business ⎯⎯⎯⎯⎯⎯⎯⎯⎯⎯

Prohibited when there is 'appreciable effect' on competition ⎯⎯⎯⎯⎯⎯⎯⎯⎯⎯

Agreement between market participants:
- To fix purchase or selling prices
- To share markets
- To limit activities
- To apply different trading conditions on similar transactions
- To impose supplementary obligations on contracts

2 Prohibition of abuse of dominant position → One where business can behave independently of competitive pressures

3 Prohibition of cartels

Cartel: agreement between businesses not to compete with each other

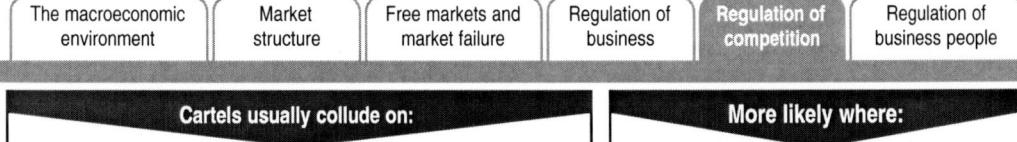

| The macroeconomic environment | Market structure | Free markets and market failure | Regulation of business | **Regulation of competition** | Regulation of business people |

Cartels usually collude on:

- Prices
- Output levels
- Discounts and credit/terms
- Technology
- 'Carving up' markets geographically
- Bid rigging

More likely where:

- Few competitors
- Homogenous products
- Established communications between competitors
- Excess capacity
- An economic recession

Competition and Markets Authority

- May investigate when one firm controls the market or when a merger involves a large amount of assets worldwide
- It reports to the government
- It seeks to promote consumer interests, competition, enterprise and efficiency
- It tries to balance rewards for innovation and the benefits of scale economies against the disadvantages of monopoly

Competition and Markets Authority (continued)

- Powers of investigation
- Imposes penalties
- Can make Competition Disqualification Orders

| The macroeconomic environment | Market structure | Free markets and market failure | Regulation of business | Regulation of competition | **Regulation of business people** |

People involved in **listed** and/or **insolvent** companies are regulated with respect to:

1 **Insider trading** – no-one may make a profit/avoid a loss on a listed company's securities on the back of 'inside knowledge' of the company's affairs.

2 **Market abuse** – people involved in the stock market must not:
- Misuse inside information
- Distort market prices
- Create a false/misleading impression about the market
- Make misleading/false/deceptive statements recklessly
- Undertake a misleading course of conduct to induce someone

3 **Fraudulent trading** – control of fraudulent behaviour in connection with an insolvent company. Person may be:
- Liable to pay company's debts
- Guilty of a criminal offence

4 **Wrongful trading** – no fraud, but person continued to trade without a realistic prospect of the company meeting its debts. Person may be:
- Liable to contribute to company assets

Disqualification of directors

- Insider trading, wrongful and fraudulent trading
- Being the director of an insolvent company
- Being unfit to act
- Being a threat to the public interest